SIGHTLESS IN SEATTLE

ADVENTURES
WITH MY GUIDE DOG

BY CLAIRE ANDERSON

With June Brasgalla

Copyright 2012

Sightless in Seattle is published by Create Space

Inquiries – Claire@claireanderson.net

Website – www.claireanderson.net
First printing October, 2012

ISBN 978-1479 106332 ISBN-13

Printed in the United States of America

Media & Reviewer Contact – claire@claireanderson.net

Cover image: Jerry Gay

Dedicated to DaVida
who has taught me
unconditional love

INTRODUCTION

When my dear friend, Claire, lost her sight at age 64, I thought her life would be severely compromised. She was such an active woman with so many interests and activities that required sight. I thought that, at best, she would lead a much more solitary and limited life and I hoped that I would be able to help her adjust.

Claire and I met in 1974 in a graduate class in counseling psychology at the University of Miami. Interestingly, the course was in Values Clarification. Our professor, Dr. Carolyn Garwood, has become a role model for both of us. Carolyn "retired" at 75 and is now nearly 10 years later one of the busiest women I know. While I went on to complete my Ph.D., Claire chose to pursue a myriad of interests beyond school. She became a quintessential entrepreneur and friend to many. Whenever we went somewhere that required long drives on daunting highways, Claire drove. When my computer gave me fits, Claire was the one who diligently appeared at my home and clambered under my desk to unravel all those usb connections. With a mere click at my keyboard, she resolved whatever had eluded me.

In the early '90s, Claire and I produced a wonderful newsletter called Transcending Limits. *Our mission statement spoke of becoming a forum for investigation and debate about the metaphysical and exploring our 6th sense. We wanted to bring psi phenomena into the mainstream. Twenty-two years ago, that was audacious and innovative! And, that is who Claire was and is. She transcends limits every day.*

It seems, really, that Claire's journey has surely been one of clarifying values. Who would have thought that this vibrant woman would ever lose her sight? As she has told me, of all the things that she ever worried about happening, blindness never even entered her mind.

Claire is a visionary. You don't need perfect eyesight for that; you need courage and determination and curiosity and clarity. In this lovely book, Claire shares her journey from devastation to joy.

Holly W. Schwartztol, Ph.D.
Psychologist, Private Practice, Miami, Florida
Past President of South Florida Writers Association
Author of Sherry and the Unseen World

SIGHTLESS IN SEATTLE

ADVENTURES
WITH MY GUIDE DOG

PART 1

Blindsided

August 4, 2005

It was the last day of my life. I was a vibrant 64-year-old woman who had a great life. I was self-employed, financially secure, proactive, and fulfilled. I had everything I needed. It was a happy day and my friend and I were singing as we drove along a country road towards Route 66 in New Mexico to attend a wedding reception for my niece. We had flown in from Miami and were marveling at the beautiful blue sky. A great day for a family party!

My vision had been a bit fuzzy when we started out driving down a country lane but I thought nothing of it. But when I came to a stop light at Route 66, I couldn't see it and didn't know whether to stop. I figured out that I had to make a left turn. I started to make a left and I realized that I could no longer see what I was doing. Waves of panic and fear flooded through my stomach and chest.

I said to Irene, "I can't see the road."

She said "Pull over!"

I said, "I can't see the side of the road."

She said what any intelligent person would say at this time, "Yaaaaeeeeh!" Frantically, she was able to give me directions, take the wheel and maneuver us to the curb.

When we came to a stop Irene asked me what was happening.

"I can't see anything." I replied.

I haven't driven a day since. My life as I had known it was over.

CHAPTER 1

The Hand You're Dealt

Irene was more shocked than I was at the turn of events at the stoplight on Route 66.

I wasn't totally surprised. I had been expecting this for more than a year. It had been predicted and I had hoped against hope that it wouldn't happen. Fifteen months previously I had lost the vision in one eye due to a rare optic stroke. My doctors told me I had a 30% chance of losing the vision in the other eye. I figured the doctors were being negative. I chose to believe I had a 70% chance of it not happening.

When my left eye went blind I continued life as usual, taking advantage of good vision in one eye. I still had enough vision in the right eye to read, drive, use a computer, run several businesses and I assumed that life would continue as usual.

Suddenly, there it was! Bam! Reality! I was blind.

With my kind of condition one usually loses sight due to a stroke which may happen as you wake up in the morning or as you put your feet on the floor. It is due to a very low blood pressure. So I probably started losing my sight in the early morning but it was not complete until I was driving.

We were both dumbfounded. We didn't know what else to do except to continue on to the reception, Irene driving of course. When we arrived and told the family what had happened, it completely disrupted the reception, as you might expect. It was the consensus of many guests that I should get to a lower altitude as soon as possible, as the stroke might have been caused by the altitude. Santa Fe is at 7500 feet. We left the party, packed up and scooted out of town quickly. We got down to Albuquerque, as low as we could prior to getting a flight back to Miami.

I was in a bit of a shock, sad, but not dysfunctional. I have always been a practical person, not easily daunted by setbacks. As we pulled in to the parking lot of our hotel in Albuquerque I saw a sign and I asked Irene what it said. She said that it was for a bus that would take hotel guests to a casino. There was still some joy in my world. Yeah! My favorite entertainment had just made itself known. I decided to go gambling after dinner. Our plane did not leave until the next morning and I was feeling fine otherwise. That is the stoic in me!

After dinner I got on the casino bus. Irene thought I was crazy and would not let me go alone even though she dislikes casinos. We got to the casino and I started to play blackjack. (The dealer would tell me what cards were down). Once Irene realized that I was safe and could return on the same bus she left me playing at the casino and went back to the hotel. I played and played. I was so happy that I momentarily forgot my plight. Irene could not believe what I was doing. She said that if she had lost her sight that day she would be crying and freaking out yet here I was at the casino playing blackjack. I lost $60 but was so happy I could still do something unaided.

The next day we flew home and I went immediately to the world renowned Bascom Palmer Eye Institute in Miami. Upon examination, there was some question about whether

I had a condition called Giant Cell Arteritis, which is fatal. I was put on the steroid prednisone and scheduled for surgery. Two wet-behind-the-ears neuro-ophthalmic residents opened me up and looked at the artery. In their infinite wisdom, they said it would take two weeks to know whether I had a fatal condition or not.

Upon release, I went home where the drugs began to wear off and hysteria took their place.

CHAPTER 2

Red Feather Boa

In my early 60s I was happily pursuing the American dream. Living in Miami and working in four occupations simultaneously, my life was grand. I had owned an accounting firm for 25 years. I worked as the executive director of a number of alumni clubs, was a life coach with clients who struggled with attention deficit disorder, and also owned a computer firm that specialized in untangling computer-accounting messes. My business and my active social life made me a happy person.

No more! Now the world was blurry and filled with gray shapes. From the exhilarating, fun-filled life, I was now in a trough, sitting on my sofa, crying. My friends came to visit and held my hand, but were at a loss as to how to help me. We cried together, but sympathy is a short-lived emotion. Friends can't sustain the intense caring forever. Plus, it keeps you in a state of suspended non-activity.

Life was suddenly very frustrating. I couldn't find food in the refrigerator. I couldn't get to the supermarket. I was afraid to cook. I ate lots of cold food. I was totally dependent on others, I felt like a useless slug.

I was overwhelmed with the fear that I might die on top of the misery of losing my sight and I was so unused to asking for help. I had been the strong one for my friends. They had relied on me. I had been such a happily independent successful person. I didn't know how to cope with the grief I was experiencing over the loss of my normal life. And, the even scarier thought that I might really be dying.

One day, one of my friends told me that she was proud of how I was handling things. I broke down and told her that I was tired of having to be so brave, that inside I was a trembling jumble. She seemed surprised to hear this; I had learned early in life to put on a good face no matter what might be happening, but this was just too much. She listened as I poured out my sorrow. She was in pain too, seeing me so distressed. I was so frightened and I was frightened of being frightened. But, I was also determined to pull myself out of my terror. Only, my stomach tightened every time I thought about my predicament. How was I ever going to feel okay again?

I felt wedded to my sofa, completely unable to fathom life without sight. I couldn't imagine putting one foot in front of another and turning this nightmare off. I was immobilized. And, I was ashamed of my neediness. The challenges ahead seemed completely daunting.

The books that I had read in my childhood had strongly affected me, and they came back to mind. "Robinson Crusoe," "Swiss Family Robinson," "Kon-Tiki," Helen Keller's autobiography, "The Diary of Anne Frank," and "The Conquest of Mt. Everest" had inspired me. I had always thought that if trouble befell me I would overcome any disaster. Now the test had come and I vowed to manage. I listened to an audio of Viktor Frankl's "Man's Search for Meaning," and this reassured me that I could go on. My life was not so terrible.

If I was a "sad-sack" all the time, my dear friends would soon drop off. If I was to have a social life and laughter, it was up to me to change my outlook.

I mused about what I had in my personality that had attracted so many friends. It seemed important to figure out what would keep my friends from sliding away; they had always described me as "game for anything." That is, if someone was going to try a new ethnic restaurant, they could count me in. Going to a spa hotel for a few days? Okay, I'm in. Freeport for the weekend, I'm there. A movie, party, book club, whatever, count me in. For many years I carried a molting red feather boa in the trunk of my car just in case a party should arise unexpectedly. I would be there, molting red feathers at the ready.

I wondered if that fun, lively person could be recreated out of this crying blob? I vowed to recreate that person. I didn't know how I would do it, nor how long it would take. Along with learning to be a competent blind person I had to become happy, funny and interesting again. Wow! This was going to be some trip.

A few days later the hospital called to tell me that I didn't have Giant Cell Arteritis. I was not going to die, I was only blind. Yeah! I got off the sofa, stood up, and got to work figuring out how I was going to live my life from that day forward.

CHAPTER 3

Not Dying, Just Blind

Even though I pulled on my imaginary Super Woman cape, added my laughing personality, and set off to conquer the traumatic event that had changed my life, there were still some crying periods.

I was thrown into reluctant retirement. With the end of driving and all of my carefully developed businesses I saw my financial future crumbling, and my independence gone. Eventually I had to call my business clients to tell them all that I could not work for them anymore. I reminded myself I was not a morbid person. I just needed to figure out how to make lemonade out of the lemons that I had been handed.

I called the Miami Lighthouse for the Blind and had a sudden resurgence of hope. They said they could absolutely help me; in retrospect I believe Lighthouse is what saved my life.

When I first called Miami Lighthouse for the Blind I didn't even know there were different definitions of what it meant to be blind. I learned that I was considered low vision and yet still legally blind. I suppose you could say that not only couldn't I read a single letter on the eye chart but I wouldn't have been able to tell you what wall it was on.

A few days after I called them, a mini-bus picked me up and I began to learn how to live as an independent blind person. I was enrolled in classes for personal care — how to dress, cook, sew; a class in mobility to learn how to get around with a white cane; a computer class; a technology class to learn how to use blind accessible equipment. It was tough going, but I persevered as if my life depended on succeeding. In fact, it did.

When I was first issued a white cane I recoiled. Shame flooded my body. Now everybody would know. As difficult as it was for me to accept my inferior sight, I never wanted to meet up with someone who had previously known me as competent. Now my disability was out there for all to see and to pity. Horror, shame, humility assailed me. No, I would not use a cane.

My patient teacher just continued on, challenging me to get down the block and across the street. I stretched to the challenge. Soon I was walking on my own and feeling so smug. I could get around all by myself. These ricocheting emotions seemed to continue forever. Sometimes I felt sorry for myself because I had to ask for help. Then I was thrilled as I accomplished something on my own.

In computer class I asked one of my computer teachers, who was blind as were most of the staff, "When will I ever be happy again?"

"Two years," he said. Such a long time, I thought, but he was right. One day, years later, laughing with my friends, I looked back, remembering what he said. He was so right.

The Miami Lighthouse for the Blind has a goal of independent living for all its students. This was just what I needed. I was lucky to live a short distance from this wonderful facility. Many students and blind teachers traveled long distances to get to school. I took to the studies hungrily, practically absorbing the lessons through my pores. I especially liked the exercise we did with a marvelous trainer named Joe. He taught me strength training so that my back would stop hurting, and he gave me balance exercises so that I did not lose my balance when I was out walking. Although I had a class schedule, there were times when I did not go to class. Sometimes I would get into a discussion with somebody and it was so interesting that I just didn't go to my next class.

One day my counselor called me into her room and sat me down. I thought, "Oh, no, they're going to throw me out for skipping classes." I was so worried. I had started to really enjoy the computer classes and just being at the Lighthouse with people like me.

My counselor Sylvia said, "No, we are not throwing you out. It's just the opposite — we are giving you an award for being the student who has accomplished the most this year with computers. The Rotary Club will be giving you an award next week at a luncheon."

I was so amazed and thrilled. This was the first of a number of awards. My exercise teacher chose me as the student who had accomplished the most in exercise class. This was really a shock to me. Here I was — a 65-year-old, chubby, blind woman and I was receiving an award for my exercise diligence. There was an article about me and my exercise teacher, Joe, in the Miami Herald. This was followed by a television show where we simulated the blind exercises we did. We also did a local radio show. The newspaper article went national and I got a call from my cousin in Connecticut who said that she had opened her newspaper and there I was exercising in the blind school. I saved all of these articles and pictures-- I'm so proud to have a scrapbook of me!

I went from not wanting to be seen with a white cane to realizing that I would be lost without it.

CHAPTER 4

Guide Guy

It was New Year's weekend, mere months since my vision loss, and I had agreed to walk with my friends in the Coconut Grove parade known as The King Mango Strut. The parade was started in 1982 by Glenn Terry and the late Bill Dobson as a parody of the annual King Orange Jamboree Parade for the Orange Bowl. After a group of Grove residents, known as the "Mango Marching Band" were denied entry into the Orange Bowl parade due to "unsuitable instruments" such as kazoos and conch shells, they decided to create their own parade.

This hilarious parade parodies local and some national news. My group was protesting FEMA's management of Katrina's devastation in New Orleans. I was dressed unglamorously with a yellow hard hat, a blue tarpaulin for a cape and my white blind person's cane. The blue tarpaulin was a reference to the hurricane aftermath, when houses lost their roofs and had to be covered with blue tarps.

While we waited for the parade to start I sat on the curb under a tree next to a motorcycle. This motorcycle ended up playing a big part in the next drama in my life. The motorcycle owner came over, sat next to me and asked if I was blind. I said, "Yes." And the gentleman said "Do you want to feel my face?"

Without answering I leaned over and ran my hands all over his face. He had a sweet beard that was as soft as baby hair.

We struck up a friendship, ended up walking the parade together and commingled our groups. As I lived three blocks from the location of the parade, Ted walked me home. The next week I climbed on a motorcycle and a slow ride to the park. That was my first and last motorcycle ride. I didn't like the motorcycle. It seemed like way too much air around me, but I liked Ted.

We continued dating for a year, ending when I left Miami. I was astounded to find that I was still attractive to the male gender, white cane and all that jazz. I never went on another motorcycle ride though, preferring his Jeep. I met a lot of bikers that year. Many of the bikers collected motorcycles. Ted had eight motorcycles. A few of the motorcycles were for parts for the other working bikes. One or two were gifts from widows of bikers. That tells a story! Some of his friends had 12 or 20. I kidded them, explaining, "You know, they are not tea cups!" They laughed at me for not understanding. This must be a guy thing.

Ted called himself "guide guy." He had a degree in history and loved museums and exhibits. When we went to Fairchild Tropical Gardens he read all the hundreds of signs on the plants and trees while I touched the plants and smelled the flowers.

Another time we went to the Museum of Science to see the traveling exhibit of artifacts from the Titanic that went down on her maiden voyage, April 15, 1912. Ted described all the items in the glass cases including a man's wallet and the money that had been in it. I was transfixed by a deck of cards with the cards intact after over seven decades at the bottom of the sea. There were cases of dishes with all dishes intact. I was able to touch some of the parts of the ship as Ted read every descriptive sign. What a good "guide guy" he was.

This relationship was a great morale booster and I thank Ted for his discrimination in choosing a cute blind woman for his dating partner. Now, several times a year he sends me pictures of his grandbaby and his new bike. I give special thanks to Ted for restoring my slightly warped feminine view of myself.

CHAPTER 5

Must Love Dogs

After losing my sight, people asked me if I was considering getting a guide dog. That seemed like a fantasy. I didn't know anyone with a dog, and I wasn't even sure that I liked dogs. Who would give me a dog when I had some vision? I wasn't totally blind. I could tell a person from a chair. True, I couldn't tell a fork from a spoon without touching them, but how was a dog to help with that? I was terrified of the venture. I had never had a dog before, just cats. I also heard from a fit, strong man with a guide dog that Guide Dog Boot Camp was the most difficult thing he had ever done. (It was clear that he had never delivered a baby).

The director of the Miami Lighthouse for the Blind had a guide dog and she encouraged me to apply. She recommended two schools, Guiding Eyes for the Blind in Yorktown Heights, New York and Guide Dogs for the Blind in San Rafael, California.

Applying to get a guide dog was similar to applying to college. There were many requirements. I was afraid I would get rejected and, at the same time, fearful of being accepted. Cats had ruled my life. Would I like a dog? Would the partnership work? Would the dog like me? What if...? What if I got sick? What if the dog got sick? How would it work? Oh my!!

I learned that I would have to go away for four weeks of training and that totally terrified me as well. Here I was blind and I would have to navigate the world of camp all alone. As a child, sleep-away camp at the age of eleven had been a lonely, tearful time. I was afraid of even the words "boot camp." I filled out the applications for both schools with great doubt. If they would just bring a dog and leave it at the door, that would be fine with me. The thought of camp made my stomach churn. Still, I moved forward.

The paperwork involved a physical from my personal doctor stating that I was in good physical shape, and a letter from my eye doctor stating I was legally blind. Then I had to acquire three letters of personal references for each application. Pages of questions were filled out and off the applications went.

They were so serious about this application process. A counselor flew from California to Miami to meet me. The home interview awed me. Even college or job applications don't include a home interview. However, I survived this part of the process.

Since I had some sight, I was sure that I would not be accepted, and that would be a relief. Soon I heard from Guiding Eyes for the Blind with a rejection letter. I relaxed. Several weeks later I got a letter of acceptance from Guide Dogs for the Blind in California. Wow!

CHAPTER 6

Country Criss-Cross

White cane in hand, I had started a new life. Each of my three sons asked me to move to one of the cities where they lived, ostensibly to keep an eye on me. My sons lived respectively in New York City, Orlando, and Seattle. I didn't consider Orlando as it doesn't have a good bus system. I visited both New York and Seattle for several weeks each to consider living there.

New York is manageable if you have a lot of courage. It's like an obstacle course. There are several staircases down to the subway, after you've figured out which line to take. The stops are announced but it was so crowded that I wasn't sure I could get out in time. Then I had to find one of the many staircases up to the street. Crossing 6th Avenue is a joke. Six or seven lanes all going the same way with taxis racing uptown. I took my life in my hands to get across. Many disabled people live in New York City, and they manage the maze. I suppose I could do it. My stress level was so high that I couldn't relax.

Next, I went to test out Seattle. I had always heard that the weather was "yucky." Many days in a row are cloudy and grey. But the people were wonderful, and the bus service superb. There are crosswalks every few blocks for crossing the street, quite different from crossing the street in New York City. I chose Seattle as my new home -- an easy choice after having seen both cities. I loved the city and looked forward to being with my family who could bring me new life and help with difficult tasks.

Back in Miami, I called on the help of everyone I could draft into the daunting task of moving. I packed up, tossed out, and donated my life. I gave over a thousand books to the library. I kept six books. Three months later I flew to my new home, a retirement center, thinking I needed cocooning. I wasn't quite ready to tap-tap-tap my way around a strange city.

The retirement center, while one of the best in Seattle, was filled with much older people. Most residents were 20 years my senior. I thought about living there for the rest of my life and recoiled. No, no, that wouldn't happen. I was the liveliest one of the group and I kept them in stitches. Then there was the food. No pizza, no Chinese, no Thai, no Japanese, no Mexican. The only food was bland American.

What I needed was my own place to live. Thinking of moving to an apartment of my own pleased me and tired me at the same time.

CHAPTER 7

Two Duffel Bags

The settlement process at the retirement home in Seattle took my mind off guide dogs for a while. One day in January, my son, Russ, met Kyle, a man with a guide dog, and asked him to call me. Kyle did more than that. He traveled across Seattle at night with his guide dog on a Metro bus to meet with me. I was so impressed that a totally blind man could do so much that it renewed my decision to get a dog. I called Guide Dogs for the Blind to see if I could still participate. Once again they sent a counselor from California to interview me and see my living quarters. In February I was approved again. Now I was truly committed to going to Guide Dog Boot Camp.

I asked the counselor at Guide Dogs for the Blind if they could give me an easy-to-manage dog. They told me if I was willing to wait until July I could get the type of dog I wanted. I agreed and settled down to wait for summer. June arrived way too fast. What I was already calling Doggy Boot Camp loomed. Years later, my stomach still lurches as I remember the anxiety of this time.

I read over the Guide Dogs for the Blind website:

"In 1947, the school moved to our present 11-acre location in San Rafael, California, 20 miles north of San Francisco. In October of 1995, we held the first graduation at our new campus in Boring, Oregon, and 25 miles east of Portland. We have graduated more than 10,000 teams since our beginnings in 1942."

Guide Dogs for the Blind sent me a ticket for July 1st and a list of instructions. I would be there for 28 days. I packed clothes for warm days and cool nights. I had two duffel bags and kept packing them and weighing them as the weight limit was 50 pounds each. I have never been a light packer. I was heading to what seemed a very foreign place for a long time and I was scared. With great trepidation I was on my way.

PART 2

Guide Dog Boot Camp Journal

Greetings from ✈
SAN RAFAEL
CALIFORNIA

Day One: I have arrived.

The plane ride to California was easy. I was accompanied by an airline attendant. But I was already thinking about the return trip with a dog in tow. As soon as we touched down in California the counselors from Guide Dogs for the Blind were there. No time to panic. We were herded to a table at an airport cafeteria where we waited together as other students arrived from all over the country.

The groups started to form right there in the cafeteria. There were many teenagers as July is the ideal month for blind high school grads to get their first guide dogs. The only other grownup was Michael from Austria. He was there to get a replacement dog. His former dog had become so attached to his two children that the dog cried every morning when Michael wanted to take the dog to guide him to work. Immediately I started to get a picture of the many and various guide dog stories.

Finally we had all arrived and we were guided out of the airport to a van. Michael was a highly technical blind man; using a GPS, he told us where we were on the bus and how close we were getting to the school. He was more informative than the bus driver, and Michael is totally blind. He also has things like a telephone with a GPS built into it, an MP3 player, and everything else I could possibly want. He is going to show me all kinds of great technology. Onward to San Rafael. My adventure had started.

Soon we arrived at the campus. Each of us was assigned a volunteer who escorted us all over and oriented us to the facility. We were shown the dining hall (very important!), the laundry, library, vending machine with Braille labels, and the central meeting room. Everyone was so helpful that my original anxiety was somewhat calmed. I thought that I might actually be up to the challenge.

The campus was extremely large with beautifully sculpted grounds, and multi-purpose buildings. Many were kennels. We would not get our dogs until two days from now. Such suspense!

At dinner the first night one of the blind teenage boys told me that there was a mall across from the school. He had been to the mall and it was easy to get there. All I had to do was go to the exit of the campus, walk about a block to the traffic light, cross the street and voila, there was the mall. I marveled at his courage. I had no idea where the exit of the campus was located. I spent the first afternoon in my room, trying to locate my pajamas and this young man was making his way out and about. What a difference there is between a teenager and a grandma!

How different is perspective. I had come from a retirement home where I was the youngest resident by 20 years, as many of the residents are in their late 80s. Now I am in camp, the oldest person in the building. My life is filled with extremes and I am fascinated.

Almost everybody has a sparse room that they share. Due to the fact that I told them that I snore they gave me my own room. I am very happy about that, as I can sit here and dictate without disturbing a roommate. All the class lectures were given to us tonight on six CDs and a CD player. Therefore we do not have to take notes and can play them over and over again. For tonight, I have my CDs to listen to. Just 20 minutes or so for tonight. The class is extremely exuberant, as one would expect from young people, and it is fun. They are as excited and nervous as I am, mostly excited and happy. This is going to be a lot of fun.

Guide Dogs for the Blind distribute approximately 350 dogs a year to the students who come here. The average dog is worth over $75,000 as the school has a budget of over $24 million.

There is absolutely no charge to students. They sent me plane tickets and everything here is part of the program. The school is totally supported with grants and donations, as it has been here for many decades. In fact, they treat me so well here that I am thinking of moving in and living here! In addition to three fabulous meals a day, many staff members come by and say, "Is everything all right, what can I do for you?" We are all treated like honored guests.

Day Two: Fakes and loaners.

Today we worked out with a fake dog. You are wondering, I am sure, what a fake dog looks like! It is a rolled up piece of towel and sort of feels like a dog with a harness and a leash on it. A person holds onto it and makes believe they are a dog and then I walk down the hall, giving it commands. This dog is called "Juno." He is not particularly obedient!

Later on, we got real dogs. These were not the dogs that we will take home, just some puppies, not fully trained, so they were weak. Practicing our skills was challenging. At one point, the dog was turned around, and I didn't even know. I could feel the dog on my left, and it seemed to be in position, but it was facing in the wrong direction. I felt so silly giving instructions to the dog's tail! This is because they blindfolded me for the exercise, because they say that it will give me better skills if I learn to do all the work as a totally blind person. I hate being blindfolded and I am in terror when I'm totally in the dark. I feel extremely disoriented and am afraid of falling. So even though they may think it is good for me, I don't agree.

Tomorrow is July 4th and we are working all day as regular students. I don't mind but I feel sorry for the instructors who do not get a day off. What they told us was that if we had a day off we would get our dogs one day later. It is hard enough waiting until Thursday to meet the dogs, but at least there is a yoga class tonight.

Day Three: I have my dog!

Suzanne is right below my desk. She is a beautiful yellow lab, almost two years old and very darling. She was so excited and overwrought at first. When she met me she was panting and couldn't calm down. The first thing I did was give her a Reiki treatment. Ever since then, she has been the perfect dog. Many of the other students are having trouble with their dogs, but not me.

Shortly after we received our dogs and spent some time getting used to each other, we all went to dinner. There were fourteen new students with their new dogs. It went mostly well but some of the students who were accustomed to using canes got a bit turned around in the dining room. One guy was facing a corner. I had to rescue him as he did not know where he was. After everybody got seated, all fourteen of us ate dinner with no incident, except that someone stepped on my dog's tail on the way in. Suzanne was not hurt. We will be taught over and over how important it is to protect the health and safety of our dogs.

After dinner we had a grooming lesson and we were taught how to brush our dogs. They said that if we brushed the dogs every day, the dogs did not have to be bathed more than once every two or three months. Bathing dogs irritates their skin and brushing them is the best thing that can be done for them. I have heard this before from another guide dog user and was not surprised to hear it again here. It does sound unbelievable, but these are professionals.

I had lunch with one of the vets from the kennels here and learned some very interesting information. They breed 350 dogs a year at this facility. They are always careful to achieve the perfect blend of dog: that is, healthy, intelligent, strong, and of mild temperament. I have not heard a dog bark today. Isn't that amazing? The vet told me that they inspect the dogs extremely carefully before they are allowed into the program. The dogs are x-rayed and all of their bones and joints are checked to make sure they have no pre-existing conditions. In addition, they check their heart, liver and lungs and all their other functions to make sure they are in optimal condition. Dogs that do not pass all the health, temperament and intelligence tests are given to people as pets. There is a long waiting list for these dogs, because even though they may not pass the test as an optimal dog, they make wonderful pets since they are so well bred.

You probably won't want to hear this, but I will tell you anyway. Just skip over the paragraph if you are not interested in bathroom habits. The main accomplishment of today was to get one's dog to poop. I am proud to say that even though many other students were in despair, because they could not get their dog to poop, my dog pooped twice. I was very proud. I think I owe it to the Reiki treatment, which calmed her and gave her lots of good healing energy. I would like to take some credit for it too, as I am extremely calm with her and patient and loving.

She is a great licker! All my sun block and makeup was licked off. I haven't decided whether to cure her of licking my face or should I give up makeup and trying to look cute? I will have to discuss this major item with the instructors. I have the best dog in the school, for sure, and she is sound asleep on the floor next to my computer, so we are both happy.

The dogs are kept in what is called lockdown, which means that there is a steel chain connected to the wall. And when she is sleeping or alone in the room, she is always connected to this. All other times, she is on a leash, connected to me. Other than times when I take her to a gated area and allow her to run loose, she is always connected to me. This will be for at least two months, as we become a team. I am leader, Alpha; she is the guide, and we are called a team.

Day Four: They call this a game?

This morning, we played a game called survivor. Actually, the school calls it traffic control or some such thing. But I named it survivor. We went out walking, as usual, but with an instructor right there. Another instructor was in a van and kept pulling in front of us, pulling out of driveways, parking on the sidewalk, and all kinds of driving hazards. It was the job of my dog to not let me walk into any of these. When we came to a car, in this case a van, sticking half in and half out of a driveway, and its back half out on the street, the dog had to get me around it safely.

There were about six different incidents where the van tried to get me. In each case, my dog did a great job of stopping me from going forward. In some cases, I even had my eyes closed and still did not hit the van. The instructor told me that the dog might be a bit super cautious in the afternoon, which I noticed. When we took our six block walk in the afternoon she was walking at a much slower pace and kept looking for a van every time we crossed a driveway. She was pretty slow, and I let her be cautious. I much prefer a cautious dog.

Some of the questions that have come up are: what is the application process like, how do blind people handle the poop and find it to pick it up, and what's happening. In answer to the second question, we do not yet have to pick it up. We all relieve the dog in a place that is like a parking circle. We are each assigned a spot about 15 feet wide and 15 feet long, and we walk back and forth as the dog walks around and around and eventually the dog goes. If we don't know that the dog has done its job, there are watchers who tell us. There have been very few incidents, but there have been a few, of stepping into it. That is enough on that topic.

It is an interesting experience to be visually impaired. If one of you walked over to the mall to get your nails done, it would not be considered an accomplishment. I get praise and accolades for doing the usual daily tasks. It certainly appeals to my show-off nature.

One of the students, a young one, bought a can of Dr. Pepper and told his dog to bite into it. I was not there, but heard about the incident. The dog bit into the soda can, and there was Dr. Pepper everywhere. Oh, to be 18 again. I'm not sure I would want to be. It is fun to be my age and having this adventure.

Another story which is circulating is about one of the instructors. He decided to get on the treadmill and do some running. After he was running, he thought that he could let go of the side bars. He let go and lost his balance and the treadmill threw him into the soda machine. There are probably more hi-jinks here, because of the average age of young students.

Now I am back in my room and waiting for an instructor to take me down to the paddock. This is a grassy enclosed area which is totally enclosed by a fence and has a gate. One student at a time is taken down there with her guide dog which is allowed to run loose. That is, the guide dog runs loose, not me. I don't even know how to play with the dog. But I will learn. We are already dancing and singing in my room. We will soon learn how to play.

Now that I am here I understand better about the rigorous application process. When I applied over a year ago, I still lived in Miami. I had to have three personal references. Then they called the personal references to really check them. In addition, I had to have documents from my eye doctor to prove that I was blind. Can you imagine someone faking it just to get here? But I did have my doctor's statements and the documents. I also had to prove that I had graduated from a mobility program such as the one at the Miami Lighthouse for the Blind. I had to have a physical to show that I was physically fit enough to do this. It is pretty grueling, as you can see.

When the instructor flew from California to Miami they checked out my home to make sure that it was adequate for a dog to live in. We walked around the neighborhood together, and I had to prove that I was mobile enough and able to know where I am. One has to give the dog directions as the dog does not know where to go. It only guides you around garbage pails, sometimes, and to the curb. When we get to the curb I have to tell the dog whether we are going forward or to the left or to the right. I had to prove that I knew my own neighborhood.

While waiting for my house and lifestyle to be approved for my guide dog to live in I moved to Seattle. I then had to have a physical examination from a local doctor, and another home visit to show the instructor that I knew my way around my Seattle neighborhood. I saved the letter of acceptance as I am very proud of it. I don't know how many applicants there were, but it is certainly an honor to be here.

Every day at lunch, we have a new person on staff sit with us. This staff member talks to us about another aspect of guide dog school. Today I met a person in the marketing department. I asked her about the funding for the program. She told me that they receive large donations from people and have been in business for more than 40 years. They have built up a very large portfolio, and they did very well when the stock market was doing well. Therefore, they fund a lot of this program from their own portfolio. That is, the interest and dividends from their portfolio. Many students give large donations, if they have the ability. A number of years ago they had a person who was an incredible fundraiser who basically did it for a long time and was very inspired. She built up a good portion of the portfolio. We certainly have to be thankful for such a person. They never mention money here, or fundraising or anything like that, unless we ask. I am so grateful to be here and so very humbled by this experience.

Day Five: Feed, water, repeat.

The first night baby slept through the night, no whimpering, and no problems. I probably snored, but failed to hear complaints from Suzanne about the snoring. I guess she will get used to it and think it is normal.

We were up at 6:15. This is just to give you a sample of our day: At 6:15 feed and water dogs, by 6:30 we are outside to relieve dogs. 6:40 time back in my room to brush my teeth and wash my oft-licked face, brush my teeth and brush my hair, try to look decent. 7:15 is breakfast, and we all have to get our dogs down and relaxed under the table or next to a chair by the time breakfast starts. 8:10 is our first class. I'm already exhausted and starting to fall asleep as soon as they start talking. Fortunately, many of the other people in the class have their eyes closed, as they are blind, and they don't know whether I am sleeping or listening. I'm trying to do both at the same time. At home I usually get up at 9:30. Here, I feel as if I have already put in a whole day by 9:30.

Every night, we are required to listen to a CD of the day's lectures. They tell us where to find it on the CD. It is embarrassing for me to say that I don't know how to do fast forward on this little portable CD. So if I have to listen to track three I just start at track one and listen to the whole thing. Now that I write this I realize that all I have to do is ask somebody but it is usually late at night, I am in my pajamas when I start to do this and I don't want to go out. I'll see if I can find somebody.

There was a lot to do before we got our dogs, and there is much more to do now. We have a lecture this morning at eight and then half the class is going into San Rafael to work their dogs and half will stay here. Dogs are then relieved (the euphemism for you-know-what) at eleven and then we give them water. It is interesting to me that the water is given to them at certain times of the day. They're given three cups of water and allowed to drink as much as they want. Then the water is taken away. I always thought that one had to leave water out for their dogs all the time. But things are very controlled here, I guess it is a rather fascist dog camp, but I'm trying to behave. Not doing such a good job. The most important thing is that the dog gets trained so that she listens to me.

We walked our dogs on a harness. That is, the dog walked me. Suzanne likes to walk fast, and I have to teach her to slow down. It was a nice long walk, but it was 90° out, and I was in sun hat and sunglasses, slathered in sun block – whatever amount Susanna had not licked off.

When we got back, at 11:30, she was so hot that she drank three cups of water. Now I have 20 minutes to do anything I want. Lunch is at 12:30 and then at 1:30. We relieve the dogs again, and get on the bus to go to San Rafael.

When we travel by bus the dogs have been trained to sit while traveling. It's challenging to stay in sitting position on public transportation. If the dogs lay down on a public bus or subway, there is a chance they will be stepped on. So we have to keep the dogs all sitting up. Their inclination is to slide into down position. It is our job to keep hoisting the dogs up into sit position. They keep sliding down like little kids in a restaurant.

This afternoon we were in San Rafael learning to walk in town and to cross streets. San Rafael is no longer the intimate little town that was featured in the movie "American Graffiti," filmed there in the 1970s. Today, it is a small city, complete with busy traffic, congested streets and a plethora of hazards to test the training of service dogs and their owners.

Doggy Boot Camp is so careful with our mobility exercises in San Rafael. Each student has one instructor accompanying them and there is an overall supervisor. While I've found the weather and the challenges of a new community rather daunting, I've also felt safe and cared for. Later on, the supervision will be decreased as we're more confident with our independence skills. To come across one of the students with his dog in San Rafael we might seem to be on our own, however we are counted at the beginning and end of every independent task and the instructors are constantly communicating with each other by walkie-talkie.

Suzanne and I were both exhausted after our adventure in San Rafael. We went back to the lounge and slept for an hour.

The lounge is a space, sort of a house, right in the middle of camp. It could be any doctor's office or something like that. There are three large living rooms, a kitchen where there is water and a soda machine and a bathroom. There is also a yard in the back with benches all around. They say it is a good place to groom the dog, as she has to be groomed every day. It was too hot to do anything today. So the instructors took out one student at a time. And if there were six instructors and a nurse with us, three or four instructors go out; one may be supervising, and one stays with us. It takes about two hours for the whole procedure.

When I was walking with my instructor, she also had a leash on the dog. This way she could monitor everything that was happening, and give the dog a tug when needed. There is so much to learn for me and the dog. The dog knows way more than I do at this time, as she has been trained for many months to be a guide dog, whereas I am only five days into it so far.

On the way back I discovered how to keep Suzanne in a sitting position. First of all, I give her a treat after she gets into sit position and I hold her up with my arms. She is so much more willing to do it after a treat. Many of the other dogs were melting and had to be constantly lifted into a sitting position. We returned at five. Fed, watered, and relieved Suzanne. All tasks were successful! Soon it will be time to feed and water Claire.

This is like having a newborn. Every minute of every day is taken up with care and training of the dog. I am proud of what I have accomplished, but have had very little rest. When there are a few minutes and I am not training with the dog or taking classes or dining, I go to this journal to remember what is happening. I know that if I don't do it regularly, it will all slip away to a distant memory. I only have about 20 minutes at one time when not in dog care. I am very happy to be keeping this journal for all of you and for all of the times when I will be able to remember this experience. I can't imagine when it will be easy, but my cognitive mind knows that it soon will be.

We are working on a word of the day here just for fun and to have something to talk about besides dogs. Yesterday it was my favorite word, "penultimate," and today's favorite word is "insouciant." I am not sure I spelled it right but am too tired to look it up.

There is not much time for anything else. The only actual free time we have for use during dog training classes is where there are 20 minute spaces when some other dog is being trained. We can talk to each other and sometimes I listen to a book on tape.

I am so tired. Suzanne is sound asleep and it is 7: 40 p.m. and I'm falling asleep. I have to stay awake until at least 8:30, so I can take her out to relieve her. The only time I ever felt this tired is when I worked-out for hours. But then I usually got to rest for days afterwards. Here they expect me to do this again tomorrow. What can they be thinking? Why do you think they make it so difficult? It is so grueling to start at 6: 15 in the morning and go until nine at night. I guess they have a lot to teach. No wonder graduation is such a big deal. You are so thankful to get out of here.

Good news. My "daughter-in-love," Aureole, is coming to visit this weekend. She will be here tomorrow night and spend Sunday with me and Suzanne. I am so happy! It will be such a relief to have somebody else here. I sure need a good night's sleep. I never thought the day would come when I would be in bed at 9:30 and thankful for it.

As I lie in bed thinking about the day, I realize that this is going to be quite an ordeal to have such a dog. Suzanne is always pulling at me when guiding, and I am always reprimanding. She is such a big barrel-chested dog. I thought back to early February and March, when the school called and said that if I was willing to wait until July, they would have an easy-to-manage dog for me. I was realizing that this was not an easy to manage dog. Although she was extremely loving and licked me every time I got near her, she jumped up on me and was always so full of energy that I could barely control her.

In the morning I called the staff and told them my concerns. Within an hour they were here, and suggested I try another dog. I had such mixed emotions about rejecting this dog that I had already bonded with but they simply took Suzanne away. Can you imagine trading in children so easily?

"Try this one," they said.

Then in came DaVida and I knew I was meeting my soul mate.

Day Six: DaVida darling.

I am so delighted with DaVida. She is the loveliest dog, a yellow Lab, with the same coloring as my hair, a small face, and high cheekbones. Already I can tell she is much smaller, sweeter, calmer, and more loving. She is so much smaller around her chest that they had to get her a smaller harness. I worked her hard today but she was so easy to get along with. I am so happy.

I've realized that she came to me on what is considered the luckiest day of the century, July 7, 2007 – 7/07/07. In fact, I heard on the news that somewhere in the world 777 couples were married. I am certainly looking forward to lots of luck in my new life as a member of this team.

When Aureole was here this weekend she took a picture of DaVida and me with her phone. This is the age of technological miracles. True I have another dog I need to bond with. But as the instructors have said, "It is much better for this to happen early on than several weeks later."

The work is very challenging, and today I made up my mind that I would do everything that I knew how to and do it correctly. Stepping out onto the curb with my left foot, signaling with my right hand, turning my body properly, and hoping that everything would go fine. The dog walked me into a garbage pail, a pole, and an open mailbox. So each time we had to go back and do it again. When we got to the offending object, I had to say, "DaVida, careful!" then I would back up a few steps and try it again. Then she would get it correctly. This is slow going. I can see why this takes a month to get it all working. When I make up my mind to do everything right, the dog doesn't.

Someone asked me about dogs that are rejected from the program. A dog can be rejected any time from birth all the way up to the day the program starts. Sometimes it is temperament or health. If they have an enlarged liver or heart or something like that, or anything imperfect in their body or personality, they will be rejected from becoming guide dogs. There is a waiting list for dogs that are rejected from the program and dogs that retire from the program as well.

I don't know how one becomes a puppy raiser, but I have met some and spoken to others. I am sure there is lots of information about that on the Guide Dogs for the Blind website. Some of the people that I have met here, trainers and office staff, have been puppy raisers as well. Some people raise whole litters of puppies. Imagine raising puppies until they are one year old or even older and then giving them away. A person has to have a fabulous spirit to do this. The puppy raisers I spoke to say that it is very hard to give up the puppies, but they know that it is important work that they do.

At graduation ceremony, I will meet the family that raised my dog. Speaking of graduation, my son, Russ, is flying from Seattle to San Francisco for the July 28th graduation and he will help me take DaVida home to Seattle. One of the things they do at graduation is that each dog owner gets to show the work that they have done with their dogs. I can't imagine it right now, but it must be fabulous. Instructors have told me that they all cry at graduation. They have known these dogs since the dogs were born and have trained them for months and then introduce them to the owners and train the dogs and owners, and then watch them go off into their lives as teams. It brings tears to my eyes just to imagine this scene.

Day Seven: Dining with dogs.

My friend Bev came by to visit tonight and I showed her all around the campus. One of the most fascinating sights is to see the dining room with 22 students and 22 large dogs next to each person. That is one dog per person of course. She took a picture of the dining room, because it is amazing. All the dogs flat on their bellies, some asleep, all behaving fantastically.

I showed her around the campus and the soda machine and candy machine. All the machines are done in Braille, and the washer and dryer with the settings in Braille, and the library with Braille books and audio books. I just received a package today from my son. He sent special playing cards with large numbers for people who are visually impaired like me, and also in Braille. I am dictating this e-mail to show my friend how well the dictation program works. Unfortunately, it seems to put in punctuation at the oddest places. I just want to tell my son that I got the cards and they are fantastic. We are scheduling a poker game for tomorrow night. I got hold of 200 pennies, so now we can play for pennies.

We are going to start with five card stud, because I think that is the best game to play with people who don't know how to play. After a while, we will go on to Texas Hold'em. I am very excited about teaching people how to play poker here and hope I don't get thrown out.

Today, they took us on the bus into San Rafael. We went to Starbucks and ordered coffee. The restaurant had about 10 dogs under the table all behaving and 10 of us drinking lattes and then we were given the assignment to walk back to the lounge, which was six blocks from the Starbucks. It was so interesting how they did it. They started each one of us off, and there was an instructor at every corner along the way in case people got into trouble, as some did. I got all the way back without an incident and that included passing a fire rescue team on the street with a man in a gurney and about 15 EMT guys all around him. My dog got us through that and we continued walking. I was so proud of myself. I figured that I'm ready to go home. What else could they possibly teach?

On a trip to San Francisco there was much more to learn. We were confronted with crowds of people, buses, elevators and escalators, what an experience.

Tonight we had a yoga class and I enjoyed it. I really love it here. They are so good to me and take such good care of me. Then I have moments of feeling that I have to get out of here. I still haven't been to the mall across the street from the campus and some of the students have already been. I will be there shortly. I can't take the dog yet, unless I am supervised as I was on the walk today. But I can take my cane and get across the street and go walk in the mall with my credit card. Yippee!

Today's lesson was about graduate programs. After you leave here, you can call the school and ask questions about any problems you may be having, talk to the vets, and your problems will be solved even if they have to fly somebody to my location to help me. Every year for the next three years, somebody will come to my place to help me and ask me how they can help. It is not to check up on me, but for me to get any help I need. For the life of the dog, they will always be there to help me. When the dog is aging, I will have the choice of retiring the dog but keeping her as my pet, giving it to a friend or family member, or returning it to the school. They will place it in a good home for its retirement years. Then they will give me another dog. For as long as I live, as long as I am physically able to take care of the dog and walk it and feed it and care for it, they will give me a new dog. Every time I need one. There are people here getting their third and fourth dogs. They have had a person as old as 87 years old getting a dog. What an amazing program. I think I say that at every paragraph.

Day Eight: One ice cream at a time.

DaVida is on her blanket gnawing on a bone and getting ready to go to sleep. We have had a big day. This morning we went to a very fancy residential area where the homes were worth millions. We walked around there and had to deal with lots of shrubbery. I did just fine, but my dog did not. She walked me into a shrub, where the branches were cut back around knee level but were overhanging at face level. Five times we re-worked that but she could not quite get the concept. It was better, but not perfect. She has to learn not to walk me into things. That was pretty exhausting, doing it over and over again. We don't yell at the dogs, and we don't reprimand, we just say, "Careful" and then do it again. At times like this you can see why training takes so long.

I heard that someone went to another school and got a dog in two weeks. Now that I see what goes into this, I would not be impressed at a two week graduation. It is sort of like getting an AA degree in guide dog instead of a Master's Degree.

Tonight we got all dressed up and had our pictures taken by a professional photographer with both the dog and me in one shot. We will then be given ID cards from Guide Dogs for the Blind, which we can use on airlines. Isn't that something?

After I requested a change in dog and was successful, it turned out that one of the other students had been pretty unhappy with her dog. She is a small young thing, 18 years old, and they gave her a giant dog. She did not know enough to complain and was putting up with the dog. In fact, it knocked her over a few times. Finally, when she saw how happy I was with my little dog, she requested another dog. They did not have a dog quite ready and had to quickly do all the physical testing and certification for a new dog. It took two days. She got her new dog tonight. We are many days into the program, and she is just meeting her dog. That is a pretty difficult situation for her. Here is when age and wisdom helped me. I did not suffer for a long time before discussing it. As soon as I realized I was unhappy, I tried to change the situation and did so successfully. What would you do, if you were 18 and totally blind? Her parents have protected her most of her life and she is not that good at taking care of herself, which is something one has to learn.

Another situation is brewing, with one of the students being unsure whether she wants to graduate and take a dog home. She is not sure it will work in her life. Yet she does not want to give up. So she vacillates from moment to moment, trying to decide what to do. Everyone is giving her advice, and that can make a person crazy. We will see what transpires there. I have simply given her the advice that she does not have to decide now. Even if she graduates and takes the dog home and finds out in two months or three weeks that she is unhappy with the dog, they will take it back.

Last year when I was at the Miami Lighthouse for the Blind, I requested that friends and family make donations to them. Instead of birthday presents, I would do the same for Guide Dogs for the Blind. This is one fabulous organization and is certainly life-changing for me and many others. I have already requested to become a speaker for them as they have a Speaker's Bureau. This will give me an opportunity to practice my skills learned at Toastmasters. I am excited about speaking for this organization. I have been wondering what direction my life would take and that will be one of them. Maybe I can become a traveling speaker and poker player for the blind. That sounds great.

Tonight we had our first poker game. But since the photographer was here, things got complicated. Only one person showed up, and I had a roll of pennies. He was 18 years old and totally blind, but was able to read the blind Braille cards just fine. I won almost all of his money, but did not feel bad as I had to stake him in the beginning. I think we will have more poker games in the future. But not tomorrow night as I am having a massage. I told you this was a fabulous place. Maybe I will move in and become a permanent student. Let's forget the time when I was trying to make a break for freedom. I remember that too, but as we are getting out more, and I'm feeling more freedom, it is getting less onerous.

Today I walked to Baskin Robbins with the entire class. We each set out about five minutes apart, so we do not run into each other. It must be quite a sight to be sitting at a café and every few minutes see a blind student with a dog walk by. We all ended up at the ice cream shop, and then the bus came around and picked us up. I wanted to walk back, but there was not enough time. I love walking my dog, and I love the freedom that I feel when I'm walking the dog. But I am not free to go into a store, as my absence will be noticed, and all the instructors will be looking for me.

One of the instructors is looking into a place where I can get a manicure. There is the mall right across the street from the campus and I can walk there with my cane. So as soon as I know the name of the place I can call and make an appointment. I hope they are open on Sunday. It will feel great if I can get a manicure and pedicure. Things are mighty fine right now.

Tonight we had a lecture from the major veterinarians at the kennel. They will be giving us flea treatment for the dogs and heart worm medicine and we are expected to do that once a month forever. They also talked about something called Fox disease, caused by the inhalation of a Fox Glove plant. It can be lethal to dogs, if left untreated. If the dog starts to sneeze violently, we have to take the dog to the vet right away and have it surgically removed. That sounds pretty bad.

Having had a cat, I know that sometimes one has to go to the vet. I think one goes to the vet a lot more with dogs. This school gives me a credit of $250 a year for vet bills and all I have to do is send in the bills and they will either pay them or reimburse me if I have paid them. This is simply a fabulous place. Some of the students have said that there are vets who do all the guide dog work for free. The same is true for some groomers. There certainly are a lot of perks to being blind. I never thought I would say that.

Day Nine: I am losing it.

In addition to me washing, brushing my teeth, flossing my teeth, doing my laundry, my hair and my nails, I now have to add grooming the dog every day, cleaning the dog's ears once a week with non-alcoholic baby wipes and brushing the dog's teeth once a week. I just got that task demonstrated to me, pretty disgusting. Anybody who thinks that after they have touched a dog they have to wash their hands would have a skin condition. After almost every single activity, that is at least 150 times a day, we pet the dog on her head and tell her she's doing a great job. If I washed my hands every time, my skin would be peeling off.

I got to thinking about the poop, and the teeth care, and the ear cleaning, and the daily grooming, and that these people are spending $75,000 to give me a companion. Is there another Annie Sullivan, Helen Keller's assistant, out there who would just love to take care of me and be my best friend for the rest of my life, who brushes her own teeth and uses a toilet and grooms herself every day? So don't you think it would be easier on me to have a 25-year-old really cute guy? If they gave him $75,000, don't you think he would like to take care of me for a few years? He would probably brush his teeth and take care of his own poop. It's just a thought. Because DaVida is getting to be a pretty high maintenance bitch. (I feel like David Sedaris writing that). Cats are really low-maintenance compared to this. But you just can't put them on a leash and go out in the streets. They are just not very good stopping at curbs.

I must get off this way of thinking. It was the tooth brushing that put me over the top. Do all you dog owners out there brush your dog's teeth? Do you groom him every day? Do you clean his ears with baby wipes, non-alcoholic? And relieve him five times a day? Are the people here crazy or is it me? You can see that so many days here is taking its toll. My irrational mind is starting to kick in. Do you think I can make a break for it with the dog?

I had better go to sleep, I am losing it.

Day Ten: Intelligent disobedience.

DaVida weighs 60 pounds and is 20 or 21 inches high. This is a very small Lab. I think she is perfect. Some of these students have dogs that they could ride with a saddle. When the dogs are lying down in the living room while we have our lectures it looks like a sea of dogs. It is amazing how well behaved they are. The biggest issue we have is that they sometimes get into licking each other and we have to separate them. That is because they have all been raised together and have been in the same kennel and sometimes having been sleeping together, not sexually, just sleeping. Some of them are brothers and sisters. They are all very fond of each other. I have never seen any of them fight or even get angry with each other.

I wish I could take pictures of these great scenes for you. I hope that the descriptions are good. The labs are mostly black or yellow, but they look white to me. My dog is quite dark yellow, and I can see that she is yellow, and she does not look white. I can see her eyes and she has the most beautiful eyes. She looks like she has dark eyeliner on. And someone told me her pupils are golden in color. She is quite exquisite.

There is a lot of discussion here about a term called "intelligent disobedience." This really appeals to me, because it is something I truly believe. You probably already know that about me. But here, it refers to a kind of dog behavior. Suppose I am standing at a curb and the light changes, and I say to my dog "forward" and she refuses to go and even though I continue to order her to go, she refuses. The reason she won't go forward is that there is a car in front of us or some other dangerous object and she knows better than I do what is safe and what is not. She is exercising "intelligent disobedience."

I have probably been exercising "intelligent disobedience" all my life. In fact, I know I have been doing so, because all my children do that and where else could they have learned it? It is a family trait and now my dog has it, too. That's how change takes place in the world. That's how women won the right to vote. That is what the Civil Rights Movement was about and many of the good things that have happened in this world. We demonstrate for what is right, and we use "intelligent disobedience" to get what we want. Good for all of us.

We had the usual walking around today and DaVida and I did fine. Then we had lectures about how to leave your dog home alone and when it is appropriate. Times to leave the dog at home are for events like fireworks and large noisy gatherings or places that will either frighten the dog or hurt them. They have done some work with zoos and have found that guide dogs do not do well at a zoo. I would never have thought of that. I actually don't go to the zoo very much. But there is a zoo one mile from my house, and it is possible that I might have arrived there one day. Some guide dogs have been so frightened at zoos that they are unable to continue to be guide dogs. It frightens the other animals and frightens the guide dogs. So if your family is going to the zoo, it is best to leave the dog at home.

The next lecture topic was not so pleasant. It was about what to do about other dogs, barking dogs, approaching dogs, and even attacking dogs. Even though this is a fact of life, I did not enjoy that lecture at all. I am sure it is good to have the information, but it is like reading about the war. Some things I don't want to hear.

I had my weekly evaluation and I got very good marks. I need some extra leash work, but basically I am doing a very good job and they are very pleased with me. It is very quiet here tonight and it is nice to have some quiet. I have gotten so used to a hectic schedule that I barely know what to do with myself when it is calmer. Then I come to this journal and write about the day.

Day Eleven: Must love dogs redux.

Talking to a friend last night, she said that I should spice up the story. Well, that is going to be challenging. The dog is neutered and come to think of it, so am I! Actually, I was wondering how I could meet somebody and possibly have a romance with a guide dog by my side. Should I run a personal ad? "Half blind woman with guide dog seeking..." What? Oh I know, seeking a 25 year-old guy who would like to fetch and carry for us. I was talking to some of the younger people about putting in personal ads and internet dating and the interesting question was, should we indicate that we are blind with guide dogs or not? The vote went both ways. So I should have two different ads on two different services. So on Match.com I can say in my usual way, "I am visually impaired, so you do not have to look like Richard Gere, but you have to smell good. And, must love dogs." Then I could do another profile, on J-date for example that says the regular, "Fabulous, exciting, amazing woman, would like to meet intelligent rich and charismatic guy." Then I could see where the chips fall. Or the guys.

My friend Bob wanted to know if there is an Alumni Association of people who graduated from the school in Seattle. That would be a good place to meet somebody. I actually do not know the answer. But, you know me, if there is not one, I'll just start it.

Some interesting developments are happening: one of the students here went home yesterday. She had decided that owning a guide dog was not for her. I guess that happens from time to time. Just like when you start college and not everybody in the freshman class ends up as a graduate. There is another student who is having a very difficult time and is going to need quite a bit of extra help. But she is being very brave and persevering and I hope that she makes it. There is a lot of gossip about each other here that I often overhear at lunch. I also know that many people meet in each other's rooms and gossip.

I pretty much have given up gossip and do not participate at all. But I am curious and interested even though I wish I were not curious.

We went for a walk on the streets in San Rafael this morning. DaVida and I actually had a perfect walk with no incidents. There is a saying here that goes "wrong is wonderful" and I understand it and will explain it in a minute. But I object to that terminology. Anyone who has seen the movie "The Secret" understands what I'm talking about. But what the term means is that while we are here in school we want as many diversions and difficulties to come up so that we can practice handling them. The fact that I had a perfect walk with no problems is not particularly good for my mastery of situations. As my instructor and I discussed, I probably need some problems to handle. She said that she would see to that. Next week they will bring up DaVida's trainer and see if I can handle the dog when she sees her favorite trainer. Will I be able to handle her and get her under control when she wants to go running to her real mother? That will be a challenge good for us both.

As to the phrase, I think it should be "distractions are delightful."

I was talking to one of the marketing people and she gave me some amazing data. There are 275 staff members including this campus and the one in Portland, Oregon. Between the two campuses they distribute approximately 350 dogs in a year. That is practically one staff member per dog.

Day Twelve: Three blind mice.

Here's the rest of the story about the weekend. It was pretty quiet. We had a lesson on dog massage and all the dogs went into a trance. They talked about Reiki and chakras and different kinds of dog massage. One massage form is called T-Touch. Tellington T-Touch was developed by an internationally known animal expert, Linda Tellington-Jones. In basic terms, T-Touch is comprised of specific touches and movements that encompass health, a positive way of training and an interest to perform. It's a series of small, circular movements that help to relax the guide dog and increase its body awareness. It was fun to see 22 dogs in one room and all of them in a pleasant trance.

Later on I went out with two other blind women and walked about four blocks to Chili's to get cocktails. We left the dogs on campus, as we are not yet allowed to take them out alone. It was a very scary walk for me but they were laughing; I think they did not realize how dangerous it was. Even though it was daytime there was no sidewalk and no shoulder on the road. There was just a lane and then a ditch and then the hill to our right. We couldn't walk on the hill and we couldn't walk in the road. So we had to walk in the ditch, which was filled with leaves and things. It was pretty hairy and I was thinking about how we would get back in the dark. Fortunately, when we got to Chili's there were two other blind students there. And we all agreed to take a taxi home, even though it was four blocks. Once we decided to take a taxi, we all relaxed and had some drinks and laughed our heads off and then we all piled into a cab later. Even though four is the limit, five of us got into the cab and two of us were quite large people— really large people! It was squishy and that made us laugh even more. I gave the taxi driver a big tip for a three dollar ride and I said to him, "I'd bet you thought blind people were sad. Wasn't this fun for you?" And he agreed that it was fun.

Day Thirteen: Kibble and clicker.

On Sunday I went to the mall to get my fingers and toes polished. The mall is so close that I timed it on my watch. I could walk from the dormitory out the doors across the street and be in the mall in nine minutes and I walk very slowly. A regular sighted civilian could probably do it in four or five minutes. I felt so free and wonderful in the mall. All those real stores like The Gap made me feel just great. Now my toes and fingers look pretty cute. It was not a really great manicure and pedicure. I would give them a C+, but I am happy anyway. Glad to get the job done. Sunday is winding down, things are quiet, I am going out to empty the dog in a few minutes and then get into bed with a good audio book.

This should be a very exciting and interesting week coming up as we are going into San Francisco, doing restaurants, elevators and buildings, including the Federal Building and City Hall. Some of us are doing escalators, but not me. I do not do escalators. They actually have to put special booties on the dogs to go on escalators so they don't catch their feet, and I am not interested at all. I can go the rest of my life without an escalator and be very happy.

We have been learning a type of training which uses a distinct and consistent clicking signal to mark a desired behavior in real time and then follow that signal with a kibble reward. Because doggies understand precisely which action earned the click and their reward, they learn new behaviors quickly, easily, and enthusiastically. All the guide dogs have been trained this way and I can continue to use it to teach DaVida new behaviors like finding bus stops and how to play poker. Just kidding (about the bus stops). I just wanted to see if you are still reading. She is very good at responding to the clicker; I am not as proficient, but am trying.

Dramas here continue. One person who has been creating trouble by being very negative and gossipy about students and instructors is now a borderline student. I feel like I am living in a television series like Gossip Girl. I have not experienced these kinds of personal storms in a long time. I think it may be due to the stress of the situation, so many people of different backgrounds and ages all thrown together. It is as if we are on a lifeboat. One of the students said that if we were on a lifeboat, the formerly mentioned gossipy woman would have been thrown over by now. It will be nice when this part of it all is over. I like the training and the fascinating new things they come up with all the time like T-touch and clicker training. I don't like all the personal drama stuff, but it comes with the territory.

Day Fourteen: Five feet nothing.

Today one of the dogs became ill. They decided to give the student a new dog. She was extremely upset as she had grown to love her prior dog. Of course, it is probably the best decision on the part of the staff. Who needs to go home with a sick dog? This is the third dog replacement. I was the first one. Our little friend was the second. She is having trouble with her second dog, but she is doing okay. She is young and weighs 75 pounds and is 4 feet 10 inches. Her dog weighs almost as much as her. So you can see why she is having difficulty. I am just 5 feet but luckily for me, in this case, I have weight and girth to manage a dog. This is the first time I have been happy to have these extra pounds. Speaking of which, I thought I might be able to lose weight here, but probably not.

Day Fifteen: Freelancing.

Today we went to the courthouse and went up all those stairs leading to the main foyer. We used the elevator and I learned how to get a dog on an elevator. The answer is very quickly before the doors close. We went up and down a lot of stairs and I think I got it right. The dog is supposed to go up first ahead of me and down first ahead of me. It is a bit challenging to have a dog pulling on me as I go up or down stairs. But it would not make any sense for me to go first as my dog is supposed to be my guide.

Later in the afternoon we did freelance and I was so excited to be out on the streets alone. Well, I probably wasn't alone. There were undoubtedly instructors all over the place watching us. It is rather an Orwellian experience to know that some big brother is watching me all the time. But it is a way of staying safe as we learn the ropes. I had run out of money because I did not bring a lot of cash. I did not think I would need it. But then I have been getting a massage every week and the masseur (do they still use that term?) only takes cash. So I found a Wells Fargo Bank and talked them into giving me money. That was pretty cool. That was my freelance experience. Then I stopped for an iced coffee at one of the many coffee shops and headed back to the lounge. I sure love my freedom. I wanted to go to a supermarket and buy some fruit. The apricots and plums are just marvelous right now. But I could not find a supermarket in my zone. That is, the prescribed area that I was allowed to walk. Perhaps the zone will be enlarged in a day or so. I guess they have to keep the zone pretty tight so the instructors can be sure to cover the whole area.

We actually had to tell them where we were going before we set out so they could watch us. I will be so happy when I get home and can walk around and not have to answer to anybody. I certainly understand why I have to be good while I am here. I am thankful that they are so cautious, so that mistakes and hurt students or dogs are minimized.

Tonight we heard a speech given by Mike Higson, who is the development director here. Mike was one of the survivors of the World Trade Center on 9/11, when his guide dog guided him down 78 flights of steps and then away from the building as it was collapsing. It was an awesome story and he made a lot of news and has since become the development director here. He explained that every student here is on full scholarship and does not have to pay anything to be a student and will continue to receive graduate assistance and receive as many dogs as needed in a lifetime. He also told us we are the best walking fundraisers they have. He told us that we never know whose lives we touch, and who may be inspired to contribute to Guide dogs for the Blind just because they have met us and seen the work of our guide dogs. I was very impressed by his story and personal style.

Hearing his story threw me back to 9/11 and all that transpired around that time. It was quite sobering.

Day Sixteen: Don't forget the booties.

To give you an idea of a typical day, here's my routine. Up at 6:15, feed the dog. While she is inhaling her food, I rush and dress, brush my teeth and am out the door at 6:30 to empty the dog. Then back and make my bed and off to breakfast at 7:15. Until I got to camp I thought it was still dark out at 7:15. Our morning lectures start at 8:10, with today's lecture on the subject of dogs in difficult weather like ice and snow and hot and wet, like Seattle weather. I already ordered a raincoat for her. I don't own a raincoat myself but my guide dog will have one. There are also dog booties to order for cold weather, because if she gets salt or ice n her paws or ice she could damage them. When you have a guide dog, her health is as important as your own. They also have booties for the dog for summertime for when they are walking on hot asphalt and might burn the pads of their paws. I don't think I need those in Seattle. I don't know whether to buy them in case I go traveling in the summer and end up somewhere where the pavements are very hot. The dogs have already been trained to use these silly looking booties. I don't want people to make fun of my dog, but they probably will.

Out to empty the dogs again and onto the bus to go to a supermarket. I finally got an opportunity to buy those apricots and plums. So this is how you go through a supermarket with a guide dog, a leash, a harness, and a supermarket cart. First you pick up the dog and put the dog in the baby seat with its hind legs sticking out. Then you can push the cart and the dog won't get into any trouble.

The real way is that the dog is on my left and I hold the leash and harness in my left hand. And then I push the cart with my right hand. In the front of the cart is a sighted guide like a person who holds the cart and helps me get the food off the shelves. This is a two-person job, and it looks sort of like a parade. First the sighted guide person then the shopping cart, then me and to my left is the dog. This we could do in a Halloween Parade. All we need is a funny hat on the dog and me. I already have a funny hat. We just need one for the dog

From there we are off to the mall. Then back to campus to empty the dogs and water them. First we fill them and then we empty them, and on and on it goes.

We ate lunch and went back on the bus to San Rafael to do freelance walking around town. Before any walk in town we have to tell the instructors where we are going and they give us a time limit. Today I went to the Lighthouse Store to look at what they had for sale. All they had was stuff for blind people and really nothing for guide dogs. So tomorrow I will go to the pet store and get some dog things. I asked when we would be able to freelance and go anywhere we want and I was told that after the 28th, come graduation day, I could go anywhere I want. So that tells me!

We have three buses that are now in use. One is for the retrains, those who are here for their second and third dogs. There are two buses for the rest of us. We started out with 14 students, and now we have 12. When we go out there are students, instructors, who number four or five or six, and sometimes instructors-in-training, and always a nurse. We are quite a crew, and they use walkie-talkies to count us and report to each other so nobody gets left behind. Wherever we go, there is more than one pair of eyes watching us and we also watch out for each other. In the beginning, they guided us onto the bus and in and out of doors of the dormitory. Now, we are allowed to leave the dormitory and go down the stairs and onto the bus by ourselves.

Each day we get more and more freedom. So we learn how to do things for ourselves. It is quite ingenious how they have worked out this program to near perfection. We have been asked a number of times to make suggestions as to what would work better if we could think of it. They are always looking to do a better job.

We were back on campus by 4:30 to fill the dogs and then empty them again. Then we had dinner and an evening lecture. This lecture was about the speaker's bureau and we were encouraged to speak about the guide dog program in our neighborhood. Of course, I signed up very willingly. This is one of the reasons I have been a Toastmaster. I am anxious to talk about this program and share this marvelous experience with others. I have a great visual aid— beautiful DaVida.

Tonight is also yoga, which I enjoy very much. The stretching feels so great. They keep us so busy that there is not much time for feeling homesick or lonely. But all of the dramas continue anyway. That is probably because many of the students are 18 to 20, and they have adolescent hormones. I continue staying out of the stories. But sometimes it is impossible. The little girl, the one who weighs 75 pounds and has had two dogs, has had a lot of trouble with orientation. She basically cannot leave the lounge by herself or get anywhere in town. It was decided mutually by her and the staff that she would go home today without a dog. We are all very sad, because we were rooting for her. She needs more mobility orientation and would be a danger with the dog because she cannot find her way across the streets. So sadness is all around the dormitory tonight.

I really don't know how well I would do if I were totally blind. Many of the students here are completely in the dark yet they are walking the streets and crossing the streets and going into stores and ordering things. It's quite amazing and awesome to see this. I am very thankful that I have the bit of vision that I do have, especially with my peripheral vision. I can generally see the sidewalks and stores. I don't usually know what store it is but I can see that it is a store. Of course in my own neighborhood I know all of the stores. So I am very thankful to be only partially blind. I certainly have come a long way to be able to say that.

Day Seventeen: I need a vacation.

I have the weekend coming up, and not many plans. I can leave the campus, but I can't take the dog. That means that I can only be gone for a few hours as I have to get back to take care of her. It will be nice when I can go and take the dog and not have to worry about getting back.

I am almost too tired to sit up and couldn't even finish my breakfast this morning. I am just way too tired. This morning we are going into San Francisco and although it would be nice to sleep on the way, the bus has no shocks and the ride is so bumpy that it would be impossible to sleep. We are going to Embarcadero. Those of you who know California may know what it is, but I don't. But I think it means something about embarking, which has to do with trains as the lesson is how to do trains and platforms. Isn't it amazing (there is that word again!) that they keep coming up with something else for us to learn? I am ready to go home and yet there is still a ways to go. What more could they teach us? I feel as if I have enough information to go home. But it seems I don't.

They could make this a three-week program and let me go. But I do know that one of the things that will happen next week is that they drop us off somewhere in San Rafael with no other information and we have to get back. Don't they do that to Boy Scouts? I think they leave them in the woods for a couple of days and expect them to eat bark. Well, I won't have to eat bark; I have a credit card with me at all times. I could call a cab and have the cab take me back to the lounge. I wonder if that is legal. Wouldn't they be surprised!

I am so looking forward to graduation, to seeing my family, to going home. One of the highlights of graduation is the people who raised my puppy for one year come to the graduation.

They take the dogs away from us to go play with the puppy owners. Then as part of the graduation the puppy raisers hand the dog over to us and we get to make a speech. I understand it's all very emotional. We will get a video of the graduation.

Today at lunch, I met Steve, who is the dog placement coordinator. His job is to find a foster home for dogs of all ages from puppies to old retired dogs. It seems a very interesting job. They use a program like Access to match the needs of the people with the qualities of the dogs. For example a puppy with a hip displacement may not be appropriate for the program yet could make a wonderful puppy for someone else. There is even a program to be foster parents.

Day Eighteen: Enough obstacles!

Yesterday we did San Francisco. We had a very bumpy ride and as anticipated I couldn't sleep on the ride. I said something on the bus about my guts being knocked around. The area where we were was called Embarcadero and it is like Wall Street. It was very shady, because of all the tall buildings. At one point, I was walking along the street and it felt exactly like being in New York City, with obstacles on the street and open cellar doors with stairs leading below the ground.

One of the goals was for me to go on a train platform. Since I did not want to go down the escalator, they located an elevator and we took the elevator down to the station. As we were walking along the platform, there was a yellow strip about two feet wide. It looks like the strips they use on corners to indicate the slope for the wheelchairs. It always reminds me of Lego blocks. These are on both sides of the platform. The size is about two feet wide and bright yellow to indicate the edge of the platform.

My teacher told me to tell DaVida to make a left turn. If she had made a left she would have walked me right off the platform. I told her to make a left and she refused and continued to walk straight. This was a perfect example of intelligent disobedience. My dog passed the test. I did not get on the train, but I could have. It would have been very easy, as the train was just sitting there with doors open and I could have just walked on. But we gave that up and went back up the elevator to the street. I walked around in the city for a bit with the dog and we did just fine. I had some coffee, of course, and got on the bus for another bumpy ride back to school.

This afternoon we had another clicker class. When the clicker specialist told us how easy it was, I really didn't believe him. It is outstanding to see a dog learn something in five minutes. You start at the object that you want the dog to know, like a chair and you have the dog at the chair and click, say, "chair", and give it a treat. Then you step back one foot, say "chair," dog walks to chair, you click, give it a treat. In a few minutes, the dog learns that finding a chair will get it a reward. The clicker is so strong a training tool that one could wait a whole year and the dog will still be able to find a chair. So the clicker can be used to teach the dog to find a button on a pole at a street corner, to find the bus stop, to find a ball and bring it back, to do all kinds of things. I can use the clicker to teach the dog where my apartment is in the building. I just say to her find the door and she will find my door. She can make many distinctions.

I won't go into all the variations of the use of the clicker. I will leave it to your imagination. Do you think it can be used with family members? Probably not. As soon as I heard that clicker, I would grab it and throw it away. Then I would sock the person who is clicking at me. So there is probably a time when the clicker is not appropriate.

When we come back from any trip, the bus stops at the west end of the building. From there we are supposed to walk on a curvy road to the door, which is filled with obstacles like street signs and pails. The dog is supposed to walk around the obstacles, and then we get to the steps, go up the steps and into the building. If the dog makes a mistake we have her sit and point out the obstacle and say, "Careful!" Then we back up and start again. Sometimes there are a number of people doing backups and blind people trying to get through this obstacle course. Everybody is bumping into each other. It is a great confusion. Sometimes at the stairs there will be two or three people and their dogs, some being corrected, some backing up, and people stepping all over each other and the dogs. It would make a great movie to watch the scene as we tried to get from the bus to the door. Someday we will do it correctly. I hope it is in this lifetime.

Even though I was exhausted, I went out for dinner with my friend from Austria. He is totally blind, and so I was the guide, so to speak. Since I had already timed how long it took to get to the mall across the street, we were able to get there in a short time. We went to Applebee's for dinner. The food was only okay, but it was so nice to get away. Then we talked about normal things like politics and family and children and life. I feel like the Bird Man of Alcatraz. Only in this case, it is dogs. It will be nice to have a real life soon. We made it back from the mall with no incidents and I just fell into bed.

You may have noticed that I have not discussed dog poop and how blind people pick up their dog's poop. Well, I'm not going to tell you. It is like the chapter in the baby books about how to clean dirty diapers. If you don't have to do it, you don't have to know how to do it. If you are really curious, drop me a note and I will describe it in detail. You'll be sorry you asked.

Friday arrives early again. I am so tired. There was an earthquake during the night at 4:45. I found out about it in the morning at breakfast. Many of the people were awakened, but I was so tired that even an earthquake did not awaken me. It was a 4.2 on the Richter scale.

Day Nineteen: Don't curb me in.

Today we learned how to walk residential streets, where there are no sidewalks and lots of cars parked on the street. The dog and I learned how to find the curb and then walk along the edge of the curb. When we find a car we have to go right and around the car and back to the curb and walk along the curb until we find a car. The teachers have located a street, actually a whole neighborhood, where there are cars in front of almost every house. We walked down and around, down and around, down and around. When we arrive at a car, we are supposed to touch it to let the dog know that we have located and noticed the car. One of the students touched the car so hard that the car alarm went off. That was pretty exciting.

Day Twenty: The walls are closing in.

Back to the camp training again. This time we went to the mall and we were each given $10 from the Guide Dogs for the Blind camp to go to a restaurant with our dogs and have lunch. I went to a Chinese restaurant, which was okay. Then I was just sitting in the mall, waiting for it to be time to go and a very lovely lady came over to talk to me about the dog. She was from Estonia and she was very lonely and asked if she could pet my dog. I told her it was okay. We had a nice talk about the Estonians. This is actually one of the things that I like about having a dog. You get to talk to nice people, who you would not ordinarily speak to. The dog is the big attraction.

After lunch I had my weekly evaluation, and my teacher said that I am doing very well and so is my dog. I knew that. Other students are having troubles and you can see that they still do not have the dog completely under control. My dog is so smart that she anticipates what I want. That is not always so good, but it is good to have a smart dog. I told Larissa, my teacher, that I was so tired that I could barely function and she excused me from this afternoon's walk. I went to bed and slept all afternoon. Now I feel great, and I'm going to tackle 162 emails this evening and I'll see how far I get. The weekend is coming up, and I have nothing to do except laundry. I probably will go to see a movie at the mall across the street as I need some kind of entertainment.

This has been fascinating, and I know I've said it before, but I've had enough. I can't imagine what else they will teach us. I feel like I know everything there is to know about dogs. I am really getting tired of this place and I am exhausted. It is starting to feel like being in jail.

Day Twenty-one: A crate to call home.

Ben, my favorite instructor, told me a funny story that he calls Humpty Dumpty. One of the students was having a difficult time with a finding her way exercise. He was sitting on a stone bench on the corner quietly observing her without being noticed. As she walked he had to lean farther and farther back to keep his eye on her. All of a sudden, he fell over on his back into a plant. There was a pole on either side of him. He was stuck in this plant with his feet in the air and could not call for help because he did not want to disturb the student making her way across the street. Finally, he continued his flip, went over 180° and ended up standing on the curb. I can still see Ben in the bushes, with his feet in the air, trying to be a good teacher.

I spoke to my assistant back at the retirement center in Seattle and she told me that Dick, the representative from Guide Dogs for the Blind in Seattle, spoke at a meeting for the residents in my building. So now they are pretty well prepared for my return. The plan we have made here is that when I get back I will always have DaVida with her harness on when I am in the building. That way, the residents will not come to her to pet her as they will know better. Then I can invite individuals to meet her by inviting them into my apartment when she no longer has her harness on.

Many people in Seattle have offered to walk her but after all the training I have had to walk this dog I would not let just anybody walk her, unless they have been trained to walk a guide dog. DaVida loves to go into her harness and wags her tail and gets very excited, because it means that we are going out and that she will get to show me how smart she is. And because she always gets lots of treats and hugs when she does a good job, she loves her harness. She has two tags on her collar. One is a rabies shot tag and one is an ID tag. When dogs walk, they jingle jangle if they have these two tags. The instructors offered me a noise reducer and I accepted it. That means when she walks around, there will not be a jingle jangle sound from the tags. It is a little red fabric bag as big as a half dollar and she looks like she is wearing a present, like a Christmas dog.

Here is some information about leashes, tie-downs and dog crates: they are meant to keep her safe. She really does not mind being tied down. When she is at home, that is, in my apartment or in some place she goes regularly, for example, to my son Russ' house, she will have either a tie-down or a crate. A tie-down is a chain with a plastic cover on it so it does not twist around very much and stays pretty straight. The purpose of this is that the dog stays in one place, give or take a few feet. This is for her protection. She has her own little rug there and is very happy. The rug keeps her warm and she's not lying on a cement floor. The tie-down is good because she does not get into garbage and eat small objects that might have fallen on the floor like a safety pin or a paperclip or any other thing that could hurt her. It is mostly for her safety.

But what dogs love most of all is called a crate. Some of them are made of metal and the dog can look out. Some are like playpens, but it is still your standard doghouse with the door. The dogs prefer their crates and if left to choose they go into their crates. They feel comfortable and safe, especially if there's a nice soft bed. They can get into no harm and the owner does not have to worry. It is best for the dog to sleep there. If you go out for a few hours, it is the best place for your dog.

Before I knew this information, I used to hear about dogs that slept in crates and I thought it was mean, like caging up an animal. I no longer feel that way and am looking at a nice crate for my dog. I will have one at home with a sweet soft bed for her. Also, they have tent-like crates for traveling and camping. If I go to a hotel, I could use a pop up crate. She would be in a tent-like environment and would be feeling very happy instead of frightened in a hotel room that is unfamiliar to her.

Day Twenty-two: All pooped out.

Today is Saturday and I spent the morning sleeping. That is, after I got up at 6:10, fed, watered and walked the dog. I came back and had breakfast. I had a meeting at 8:10 for further clicker training. I finally got back to my room at 9:30 and slept until lunchtime. DaVida slept, too. She must be as tired as I am.

I spent the afternoon reading and responding to e-mails until a little doggie came along and knocked the mouse out of my hand. I wonder what she was thinking. I looked at my watch and it was four o'clock. I have been pretty much ignoring her all afternoon and so she told me.

We did dinner and then I took her to the dog park. Here we have an area that my dog can run in. Only one dog is allowed in at a time, therefore, there will be no disputes and problems and dogfights. If someone else is in there, we have to wait until they are finished. There is a 15-minute time limit. I threw her a dog ring and she ran and picked it up and brought it back. I may be able to teach her how to fetch. We stayed in the dog park for a while until she was lying down in the dirt resting and I figured that she had enough.

Tonight there is a swim. They have a lifeguard they call in if somebody wants to swim. I told them that I wanted to go swimming and so a lifeguard is coming. I guess I will have to do it. At least I will jump up and down and do some water aerobics, since I did not do anything physical today except walk the dog around in circles.

My friend Sandy asked a question: if I give DaVida a treat of kibble every time we cross the road, will I have to do that forever? We do give the dogs rewards, whenever they do something very good. It is random rewards. Usually, I don't give her kibble every time she crosses the street. But in a situation where you are counting the blocks, you could do so and not do any harm at all. When she does something very terrific, I give her two or three.

There are many distractions they set up for us here to see how our dogs will manage. They throw food on the ground to see if the dogs will pick it up. My dog never does. Sometimes they bring a group of tiny puppies through to see if they will distract the dogs while they are working and some of the dogs do get distracted. Sometimes they just take an unknown dog, like the dog of one of the teachers, and run through us while we are doing work with the dogs. If my dog stays on task during those kinds of experiences, I give her an extra reward. Sometimes I give her kibble just walking down the hall with me at my side. The trick is for it to be random so they don't function only for food. They also get lots and lots of praise and hugs and verbal rewards. If I knew all this when I was raising my children, they would have done much better in school. This is behavior modification at its finest.

I am thinking about home. There will be lots of support when I get home. We're already talking about transition, had a long lecture about it today. I had a private conference with my instructor and we discussed going home and how I will set up my house for the dog. There is also a support group in Seattle for people who have guide dogs. I know the location and it is a 15-minute bus ride from my house, near Northgate Mall in Seattle. I have been to the mall many times and it will be easy to get there.

In addition, Guide Dogs for the Blind reminded us about their graduate services. They have a phone line available day and night to call with problems. If I need extra help, they will send somebody to my home to help me solve the particular problem. Plus there are veterinarian services always available at camp. If I have to go away for a period of time I can bring the dog here and they will keep her in the kennel and take very good care of her. This is also true if I should have to go into a hospital for a while, they will take care of the dog. There is support now and always in the future. That is the best part about a school like this that has existed for 40 years and has enough of an endowment to be in existence forever.

As I was writing about the support that exists here, I was thinking there is nothing like this for parents. When you are having a child you never get this kind of training and knowledge about how to take care of the baby or what to do when you get home. There is not a place where you can call for help and where help will be available to you forever for problems that you will have. It's fabulous that it is available to me for my dog, but it surely is more important for all the millions of babies being born to parents who don't know how to take care of them.

I don't even remember getting a lesson in how to diaper a baby. We all had a copy of Dr. Spock, and that is all the information we had. "Here's your baby and go home and do a good job." So we took them home and named them "Rainbow" and "Misty." We wore bell bottom blue jeans that were patched and embroidered and we hoped for the best for our children. The 60's were fabulous for us, but maybe not for our children.

Day Twenty-three: No sex?

Every day I get up at 6:10 and race around to be out at the eliminating circle by 6:30. I must be crazy. There has got to be a better way. This adorable doggie is going to have to learn to get up at 8:00 or 8:30 and go to bed at midnight. But we will take care of that when we get home. It is too late to become rebellious. I ruined my reputation the first day I was here. In fact, it was on the bus from the airport to the campus. The counselor was sitting with us newbies and said, "I just want to remind you all that there is no alcohol, no drugs and no sex on campus." I said in a shocked voice, "No sex?" They all looked at me. They probably had shocked expressions on their faces, but I couldn't see. So you can imagine that things went downhill from there. I only saved myself by being very good at whatever they teach me.

Day Twenty-four: Did we land yet?

Today they taught us how to walk around round corners. I never even knew they had round corners until today. What will they think of next? Round corners are found in residential neighborhoods that are trying to be cute. The dog doesn't know that the street has ended and continues around the corner instead of going to the curb and allowing me to guide her across the street. As soon as I notice that we have gone around the corner instead of going straight, I have to head her off and tell her to make a left turn to the curb. Then we cross the street to the next curb. And then we have to make a left to curve around so that we can continue going straight.

Whoever came up with all these things to teach us? Before we started the round corner sidewalk exercise, we put summer booties on the dog's paws. I don't know who felt more embarrassed about dogs with booties, me or the dogs? DaVida is so willing to please, she allowed me to put on silly summer booties and walk those silly rounded curved sidewalks. Such a good dog!

Afterward, we took a very long bus ride into San Francisco to go to Union Square. Since we have lost a few students, there was a lot more room on the bus and I spread myself out on a bench seat and tried to sleep all the way into San Francisco. The bus, still without shock absorbers, felt like the worst plane ride I have ever had. When we arrived there. I said, "That was a really bumpy ride, did we land yet?"

Union Square is a very busy area with lots of people and we were set out on the street to dodge through the people and the panhandlers and the construction people to see if we could make it from one street to the next. We successfully navigated Union Square, so tomorrow they are going to take us to Fisherman's Wharf, which is more difficult. It certainly is sink or swim here. Every time I get good at something, they give me something more difficult.

Day Twenty-five: Worse than three blind mice.

There was a swim a few nights ago. Six blind swimmers are worse than three blind mice. We kept crashing into each other in the middle of the pool. It looked like feeding time in a fish tank. But we all survived. The water was lovely at 85°, but since it was night time here in California, the air was below 70° and it was dreadful getting out of the pool. I did my water aerobics, hopping up and down, and I felt so refreshed.

I must be doing all right here even though I feel like all I do is complain. There really is nothing wrong with the food here, if you like comfort food. Every night, there is something like meatloaf or beef stew or macaroni and cheese. Today they had eggs for breakfast and egg salad for lunch. In fact today I had what is called the exit interview, where they asked me to truthfully tell them my feelings about the experience. I basically told them that it was fabulous and wonderful and that I was honored to be here. The staff is terrific, and everybody wants us to succeed and does everything they can to help us succeed. But the food?

I have the same complaints about the food here that I have where I live in Seattle. The food is not at all heart-healthy. One would think that a place like this in California, where they're so forward thinking, would have lots of vegetarian choices and heart-healthy choices. They only have had fish twice since I arrived, and almost all the meals are beef or fatty foods. They have bacon or sausage almost every single day for breakfast. The battle to stay healthy and eat healthy continues. The dog gets very healthy dog food; the students get comfort food with cookies and ice cream for dessert. One day they had watermelon for dessert and I was very happy. Everybody at my table complained.

Day Twenty-six: I can see the barn!

In today's class they talked about the transition to our homes. One of the things they said really surprised me. We can give our dogs apple slices and carrots as a treat. I think that is terrific.

I told one of the teachers here that I was very tired and she suggested that I stay in this afternoon and not do a route. That is how I know that things are coming to an end. We have options. I enjoyed the choice I made this morning. We went to the airport to meet with the security people and have them show us how they can take us through security comfortably. While we were waiting, we were in two rows facing each other, 10 people with yellow labs on one side and 10 people with labs of other colors (like black) on the other side of the aisle. People were standing around and taking pictures of us all over the airport, because we were so picturesque. We didn't even plan the color schemes, we just sat down.

Security was so nice it was hard to believe they are the same people that you meet in airports elsewhere. They showed us how to get the dog to stay as we walked through the security arch. Then the dog followed and at no time did we let them off the leash.

The security personnel asked if we had any advice as to how they could do the job better. Am I dreaming? Is this real life? This is just what everybody asks you. Right? They were very nice and I'm sure that going home will be easy and pleasant. They did suggest that we get a sighted guide at the airport to help us, because once we take off our jackets and shoes and all that and put it in the basket, it would be difficult to find it on the other side of the x-ray machine. The airport was fun. When we got back we had lunch. I climbed into bed and slept all afternoon. So did DaVida.

Later I took her out to the paddock and let her run around a bit this afternoon, as she did not get much exercise. I didn't either, but it was okay with me. One of the biggest health hazards for dogs is obesity. That goes for me too. One of the students here came with a goal to lose weight. He has been on what he calls the no S diet and he has lost quite a bit of weight. The diet is simple. No snacks, no sugar, no seconds, except for Saturday, Sunday and special days. Special days are Thanksgiving Christmas, birthdays. Every time they serve dessert, he gets up and leaves the dining room. I am always in awe of someone who can plan and do it.

My problem is a philosophical problem. I have two philosophies that clash. The first is that the body is a temple and we must respect it and take care of it. The other philosophy is *carpe diem*. That is, life is short, and we don't know when something terrible will happen and we will get very sick and/or die. So grab as much fun as you can, as you go along. My two life philosophies come head to head when faced with chocolate mousse with whipped cream or Bananas Foster. That is why

I tend to be on the chubby side. Life is short. That part of the philosophy wins. I do truly believe it as well as I truly believe the "body is a temple" philosophy.

I thought with all the work that we would be doing here, there was a possibility I would lose weight. I haven't been on the scale in a month, but I know I did not. Part of the issue is I thought I would have more exercise here. When we are working with our teachers, we go out one at a time. There are 20 minutes or 30 minutes of work in the 1-1/2 hours of waiting time, while other students wait to have their turn. The work is tiring and the waiting is exhausting. During the wait time, we can't go out alone and leave the dog. We can't go out with the dog, unless we have an instructor with us.

Once I am at home, I can go out as much as I want. I'm looking forward to taking some yoga classes and finding a Pilates instructor in my neighborhood. It seems important to get thinner for my health. I'm not sure about my own attractiveness but people have been telling me that I am looking shiny and full of life. I can't see in the mirror, but I've heard it from so many people that I'm beginning to think that I am looking good in my old age. Who would've ever thought of that? Maybe it's the relaxation and much less stress than working. Maybe retirement does agree with me after all.

I know this is coming to an end as I am now thinking about handling a month's worth of mail when I get home. I'm starting to think about packing up all this stuff in my room: dog, dog stuff, all my clothes, tapes, CDs, computer. Oh, I can't stand this. It's worse thinking about it than doing it.

Tonight we are having a Toastmasters meeting in the great room. I am delighted. They even asked me to participate. This will be really good for those students who are going to participate in the speaker's bureau to see there is a place where they can have a good time and develop their speaking skills.

Tomorrow we are going to see the redwood trees. I had some allergy testing done a few months ago and it turned out that I'm not allergic to any foods, but I am allergic to redwoods. I have a slight hesitancy about going to see the redwood trees. On the other hand, when will I ever see them again? So I am taking my inhaler and going, I think. I may lose my courage in the morning. It would be terrible to have an asthma attack at this point in my experience.

Day Twenty-seven: Why risk graduation day for the redwoods?

I stayed at camp planning my graduation speech.

Day Twenty-eight: Graduation Day!

We had so many lectures and information preparing us for the last day, but nobody mentioned how exhausting it would be. In the morning of graduation day all the puppy raisers arrived. The people who raised my puppy, Jamie and Dan, drove seven hours from South Los Angeles to come to my graduation. I should say DaVida's and my graduation. When my puppy saw her puppy raisers, she went crazy. She turned in circles, she jumped, she licked them. They had raised her from eight weeks old until 16 months and it was clear all three loved each other passionately. I left my dog with Jamie and Dan and proceeded to the graduation stage.

The ceremony was amazing. All of the students were seated in a semicircle while their dogs were inside with the puppy raisers. I was the first one on stage.

I had planned a speech that I hoped would be magnificent, leading up to how I got to this place in my life. I ended with this:

"I want to tell you that this has been the greatest adventure of my life. For one thing I have met some amazing people, young and old (I'm the old one), who have persevered through a difficult program with the most wonderful dogs in the world. These dogs have been trained for two years to do nothing but make our lives better. I am so grateful and honored to be one of these people chosen to have a guide dog. The staff here has been nothing but superb and I thank each and every one of you for the marvelous jobs that you have done to bring me to this place. In this moment, I go forth with my dog, DaVida darling. I expect so many more fabulous and enchanting experiences with her. You can be sure that you will hear about it. I have been recording my experiences in a journal and there have been many requests to turn it into a book. So it will be. My heart is full of love for each and every one of you students, teachers and staff. Thank you for changing my life so that I can now say, "I am thankful I lost my vision so that I could come here and be trained and then get to go home with DaVida darling.""

Then out came DaVida, Dan and Jan. It was wonderful.

We had a small reception after the graduation and then basically got on the bus to go to the airport. I never would have made my plane if my son had not been with me. The bus ride should have been 45 minutes, but due to accidents of other cars and just California traffic, it took over two hours to get to the airport. The other three people on the bus missed their plane to San Diego.

Fortunately we had a few minutes to spare but still had to run into the airport with Russ trailing 150-pounds of luggage, me and the dog. There was a line to check-in and Russ went right to the front and said to the people: "Is anybody here going to miss their plane if they don't get ticketed right now?"

They all looked at him with blank or stunned faces, but nobody said a word. We went to the front of the line and got ticketed immediately and then we had no one in front of us at security. They did do a secure body check of both me and the dog and we raced to the plane and got right on. We were not sure that our luggage had made it, but we were on the plane.

I had a bulkhead seat and Russ was sitting in the back. He asked if somebody in the bulkhead seat would switch so that he could be in that seat with me and one of the other passengers got up and went to the back even though he had paid $30 extra to sit in the bulkhead seat. When Russ offered to give him the $30, he adamantly refused. We had one good fortune after another all the way home and when we got to Seattle our luggage was there.

DaVida slept through all the excitement, as if she were a new baby. We walked miles to Russ' car with our luggage and got home at 10:00 p.m. totally worn out. I fed the dog and took her out for a walk and was too tired to even brush my teeth before bed. Nonetheless, I had survived Doggy Boot Camp: one of the most difficult things I had ever done. The new life had begun!

PART 3

Sightless in Seattle: A Full Half Cup

CHAPTER 10:

A Full Half Cup

I am home with my beautiful dog. Now what? For the first few days all I did was feed the dog, water the dog and sleep.

After a month I realized my life was still just about caring for the dog. Like the astronauts who focused on space, I had made no plans and given no thought to life after Guide Dog camp. Must think…

I started taking Braille lessons from a friendly blind woman named Alco Canfield who lived in Ballard, a lovely section of Seattle. I took the bus to Alco's place. She met me at the bus stop and walked me to her apartment. It was so airy, bright, and convenient. I told Alco that I loved her apartment. She told me that the apartment next door was for rent. That day I met the landlady and gave her a deposit. The decision to move out of the retirement home was made in a flash. I moved into the miracle apartment, and overnight had a lively and fully functioning blind person for a neighbor.

Alco and I have become good friends. She loves cooking, makes her own bread, and she taught me to use a juicer. She helped me over many blind issues, teaching me the ropes of living in a sighted world. I will always credit Alco for the fun and the lessons. Braille lessons? I never succeeded. Braille is way too difficult for me. Maybe when I run out of other things to do I will tackle Braille?

My new home is a sweet apartment in the heart of this wonderful Seattle neighborhood. Ballard is like the East Village in New York City. There are lovely restaurants and bakeries, art shops, antique shops, thrift shops, and many banks and boutiques. I live two blocks from its center, one block from a lovely park, and one block from the Ballard Library with its living roof. That means there is grass and plants on the roof. Seattle is innovative in many areas of sustainable living. Many of the community activities take place at the Ballard Library. I am just getting to know my way around, learning the bus systems. I already have a number of friends in Ballard.

On Sunday DaVida and I walk to the award-winning Ballard Farmers Market for produce and to meet friends. Many blocks of delectable organic foods entice us as we stroll along. Once a month we attend the Ballard District meeting to find out what is happening. Several times we attend Ballard Writers workshops and other entertainments. Ballard Rotary is high in our activities as the Rotary supports the Boys and Girls Club, the Senior Center, the Ballard Food Bank, gives scholarships to students, and other needs. DaVida and I are entirely enmeshed in our community. Wherever we go, our friends stop and say "Hello" to us. What a nice life!

Once home from Guide Dog camp with its 6:15 rising, I soon delightfully returned to my former waking and sleeping routine. DaVida adapted easily. I've always been a night owl. Call it insomnia, circadian rhythms, biological time clock, whatever you will. Earlier in life it was an issue, trying to get up and go to work on a schedule that never felt like my own. Now I don't have those issues. I go to bed late, get up early, walk the dog, then go back to bed for a few hours. This is so luxurious. It feels like vacation all the time. It serves my purposes and DaVida has adapted to MY time schedule, unlike the rest of my friends!

I also read a lot. I read voraciously before I lost my vision. My friends loved to see me coming with a big box of finished books. None of them could keep up with my reading speed, so they had a continuous source of free books. I am now a fan of audio books because I can turn one on when I can't sleep and the narration helps me go back to sleep.

As I was telling my family about my audio books, my grandson asked me if I would want to have my good eyesight back. As I thought about it, I realized that it would be as much of an adjustment to restored vision as it has been the last years adjusting to being blind. I have built a whole life around being partially sighted. I am always looking for a good term to describe my condition or situation. In the medical world it is called legally blind, 20/800. In the blind community it is called low vision. I have decided to call it a half cup of vision, but it is a full half cup. My life is so filled up with accommodations and adjustments, all of which are quite terrific, and if I had my vision restored, all of this would go away.

My wonderful and loyal companion guide dog DaVida, who is the joy of my life, makes it possible for me to go anywhere and do anything. Through a variety of services, I am able to take care of myself and my home so well.

A volunteer through Community Services for the Blind comes over once every two weeks and we spend a few funny hours solving computer issues. She is so smart and has become a good friend. She helped me build a social network on my computer.

Wherever I go, people stop to talk to me about my dog and they tell me how beautiful she is. Then they tell me about their dogs and cats and how much they love dogs and cats. These conversations occur everywhere, in every situation. If I were just a regular sighted person, I would not be getting all of this attention and help. I am comforted by the help and attention I receive. It eases the fear of getting hurt when I know the people in the supermarket or at the drugstore are watching out for me.

It took me quite a while to adjust to all of the help, as I used to be extremely independent. Now I am enjoying it and so appreciative. I feel as if I am in charge and do not feel like I have lost my independence. It has been an interesting balancing act of being dependent and independent. I feel that I have accomplished it. It was not easy. The first year was extremely difficult for me as I felt that I had lost control of my life. Interestingly enough, I feel in control of my life now even with all the help I get because I can decide what each person who comes here does for me. It just feels like managing a business as I have done for many years. I am so grateful to them for being in my life and making it work.

Research says it takes two to three years to adjust to new life experiences. It has been several years since I moved to Seattle and I love it here, including the weather. Although it is often gray and dreary outside, people here are always having fun. As soon as I walk into the library or a restaurant, or my home or someone else's home, it is always warm and full of life. I actually find it easier to be outdoors here than I ever did in Miami, where it was always hot. It is so much easier to be outdoors in cool weather. The trick is to dress properly. I have an indoor/outdoor talking thermometer and I can always check what the weather is outside before I go out. Then I dress appropriately, so I can be outdoors and walk. It is a different adjustment than if I were driving around. You can keep a lightweight jacket and a heavyweight jacket in the car and switch during the day. I have to dress in layers, so I can discard a layer during the day when it warms up. Everyone carries a canvas bag or a backpack for that purpose. It is a different group of people, who travel by bus and walk. Many are executives, working people, retired people, and then there are the others. I won't dwell on this group except to say that there is a large contingency of homeless and mentally ill, who ride the buses and one has to get used to that. Enough said.

CHAPTER 11:

To work or not to work

I have been retired for seven years, legally blind for seven years, a Seattle resident for five years, and a guide dog partner for five years. Life has fallen into an easy pattern of moderately stress-free living. I am enjoying myself almost all the time. There are some periods of boredom, but that is not such a terrible problem. I never feel lonely. There are so many people, friends, family and helpers in my life.

I used to be an adrenaline junkie and still feel that need running in my blood. That is why I was running three businesses, until I lost my good eyesight. I always liked living on the edge. I still get that kick from playing poker, but it is something to explore, the need for excitement or adrenaline kicks. I think some people like the opposite, calmness and no excitement, but not me.

Sometimes I wish I was working. I would welcome work that I would love. But I do not have to work and that is nice. There are fewer work positions for a smart, half-blind, over 60-year-old woman. Sounds gruesome! Let me rephrase that. With all my experience and lack of visual acuity, I probably should start my own business. There, that sounds better. I do really well when I have my own business. It inspires me and I can spend many hours happily working. Now the question is what to do? Sell pencils from a tin cup? Too old for the oldest profession! Will I find my next career on the Web?

I have joined the health club a few blocks from here. I am studying Meditation and Buddhism, Qi Gong, (Seattle is very "woowoo") and attending Celtic Celebrations such as Autumn Equinox! I am always involved in a book discussion group or two. What do I do in my spare time? The answer is nap, of course.

Still I find myself thinking in different ways about life now that I am retired. I think of those less fortunate than I and how I can help them with my energy and my good intellect. There are so many people in need that it is quite overwhelming to decide which way to turn. I belong to four Toastmasters clubs and I have been putting my energy into helping grow the Toastmasters, including the group at the prison who are Toastmasters, and one specialty club called, "Philosophically Speaking." I am also putting energy into the Mensa group of Western Washington, into a homeless community here in Seattle, helping some of the seniors at the Unitarian Church and the Senior Center where I teach a writing class, and looking for other roles. At first, I didn't know how I could do volunteer work with my diminished eyesight. Now I know that my abilities as an organizer and leader are needed in every organization.

That is how I am now volunteering. It seems to be appreciated. All the practice of organizing dinners and speakers for the Wharton Club, the Harvard Club, the Yale Club and the Certified Financial Analysts and other clubs have helped me become an event organizer. I am able to use those abilities here. I am coming into my own in the organizations and clubs. I knew I would find myself eventually, but was unsure of how. Now that life is moving along, it seems so obvious, you just have to let life fall into place.

CHAPTER 12:

Cruising

Traveling has varied from simply delightful to terribly awful. Early in my story, with my white cane in hand I visited my son, Brian, who lived in New York City. A taxi picked me up in front of my building. The doorman handed me to the taxi driver. The taxi driver delivered me to an attendant at the airport who checked my suitcase. I was handed to a wheelchair attendant, who wheeled me to the airplane. The plane attendant took over and seated me in my seat. The plane flew nonstop to New York City where the plan was played in reverse until I got out of a cab in front of my son's building and another doorman greeted me. That was easier than going to the grocery store. I had this one good memory and it encouraged me to keep traveling.

Oh, my, some of the catastrophes still curdle my blood. The year after I got DaVida, three of my dear friends and I attempted a three-day cruise from Miami to the Bahamas. I had alerted the cruise line (which shall remain nameless) that I needed approximately 10 pieces of grass sod for the dog to relieve herself. We were onboard and just moving out of the Port of Miami. We took a walk in order to check out the "facilities" on the 10th deck. There was a 4' square box. The attendant said that this was for DaVida. This box full of woodchips might have been good for a cat, not a dog. We were out of port and there was nothing to do. We walked her around and around but DaVida is such a good dog, she was not going to relieve herself in the wrong place. All night she held. The next morning Irene took her for another walk around the deck, planning to end up at the box of wood chips. Off went Irene in her pink blingy sweat-suit, festooned with rhinestones and sandals with rhinestones. A perfect cruising outfit! As she and DaVida crossed the pool deck, covered in Astroturf, DaVida exploded with all her withheld poop. There was no one around to help and Irene didn't even have a poop-bag as she was heading for the woodchips. This was a brown horror story. Enough said.

We haven't taken another cruise together since that day. Several years later I was invited on a short cruise leaving from Seattle. I went and DaVida stayed home with one of her many friends.

The taxi ride from Hell took place in Miami. I flew with DaVida to Miami from Seattle nonstop. We sat in the bulkhead seat with lots of room for DaVida to sleep on the floor. So far so good, until I was in a taxi on my way to Bev's house. Bev had sent me street by street directions to her house. As I got in the taxi and we started driving, I handed a page of instructions to the driver. He tells me that he can't read English but he understands instructions. I tell him that I can't read either. He shrugs and tells me we will find it. I direct him to Bev's neighborhood, but now we are both lost. There are 84th Avenues, Places, Courts, Roads and Streets. Around and around we go with the meter running and running. Exasperated, I shout at the driver to pull up under a cross street and read the two streets to me. I call Bev and tell her where we are. She hops into her car, arrives where I am and guides the taxi to her house. As we tumble out, the driver asks for $60 for a $30 trip. I give him $30 and a tip about taking me out of the way. He sullenly drives off. I arrive crying and exhausted.

Every trip I get smarter. The last time I visited Bev in Miami I had the directions printed in 150 font type, which I can see. It takes 25 pages to print out one page of directions, but this time I am ready for any taxi driver. Hah!

Example of 150 point type

150

CHAPTER 13:

No kisses for Claire

One night I went to a formal dinner in the grand ballroom at the Westin Hotel. The only person I knew was my friend Steve, who had invited me as his guest. However, DaVida, my guide dog, seemed to have many friends at the event. Women came across the ballroom to greet her, dropping on their knees in their evening gowns to rub her ears. She responded with doggie kisses and to some of her favorite friends by rolling onto her back so she could get a belly rub. Then a few more doggie licks and they parted.

All evening people smiled at my dog, cooed at her, acknowledging her. I guess I was probably having one of my invisible days. The man I sat next to rubbed her head all during dinner. Me? No cranial massage for me. Just, "Pass the salt, please."

As we were leaving, one of the waiters ran across the ballroom to say, "I'm not handling food anymore. May I pet your dog?" Then there was more nose rubbing, ear massage, and kisses. She made a lot of new friends and you can be sure that if we ever meet any of those people anywhere in Seattle again, there will be a great reunion.

I, on the other hand, was introduced to a number of people, extended my hand and said, "How do you do?" as if I was Eliza Doolittle after transformation. In return they were no kisses for me, no belly rubs, no ear massages. There is a lesson here. A dog's life is made up of love and kisses, massages, and new friends made each day. The next time I meet someone I like, perhaps I will roll over on my back and ask for a belly rub. The world surely would be a different place if we all did that.

Several times a week DaVida and I walk over to our Java Bean Coffee Shop. It reminds me of "Cheers," where everyone knows your name. As we walk in we hear, "Hello Claire. Hello DaVida." DaVida gets some ear rubs and a kiss. Me? I get just the regular coffee. DaVida knows how to work this crowd. She lies down so her head is facing the bowl of dog treats on a high counter and waits for her next conquest. First, she makes eye contact with a coffee-drinker. The drinker comes over to DaVida and asks me if she can pet the dog. I assent. Now DaVida looks longingly at the dog treat container. The coffee-drinker sees this and asks me if DaVida can have a treat. "Just one-half." Score round one for DaVida. Treat daintily eaten, she starts the whole process again. I enjoy my coffee and the "DaVida Show."

Another day I was at the doctor's office and asked to use the restroom. Usually at a doctor's office or hospital the restrooms are large and DaVida goes in with me. This one was tiny. I gave her the Sit/Stay command and went in and closed the door. When I finished my business and came out she was in the same position I had left her. I was just about to reward her when the woman in the office across the hall said, "She came in my office to visit me. When she heard you coming out, she ran back and got back in the same position that you left her in."

I felt so disappointed. No treat for that! What is a mother to do?

DaVida and I are both members of Ballard Rotary. She has her picture in the Directory with her address and phone number. She has her own Membership Badge. When we get to the meeting, she "works the crowd" like a good Rotarian, greeting and kissing her Rotarian friends. She is way more popular than I am as I don't kiss all the members or stop for ear rubs and scratches. She has her favorite members (Steve, Lori, Terry) and always secures a ride home for us. Her antics are always good for a laugh. Then she remembers that she has left me unguided and unguarded and comes back and settles at my feet for the program. After lunch and the program, she reworks the room to say "Good Bye" to all her beloved friends.

Of course, every fault she has is my fault. I feel guilty that I am not a good alpha team member. She is so cute, charming, and beloved that I leave the situation as is. It's just like raising children. The parents set the boundaries and the kids work continuously to expand the box. Thank goodness for the work of Guide Dogs in training her when she was young.

CHAPTER 14:

Adventures by bus

What has been wonderful for me has been taking bus lessons. Right after I moved to Seattle I found out that the bus service (Metro) had instructors who would teach a disabled person, like me, to use the buses. I signed up immediately. I was extremely fortunate to get an instructor with a trainee. She was teaching another person to be a bus instructor. I had the pleasure of two traveling companions. They explained the system and transfer systems. There are so many routes that most people learn just enough to get from home to work. There is also a computer site with all the routes and times.

My first trip was to Capitol Hill where I attend a low vision support group, which I had been attending by taxi. I was excited to learn how to get there by bus. The tricky part is knowing when and where to get off the bus, although the bus driver usually tells you, but not always. Once off the bus I have to know whether to go around the corner, or cross the street straight or diagonally to transfer to the next bus. This part makes me nervous. What if I start off in the wrong direction? Being lost brings up my childhood fears. The transfers are always tricky. Seattle downtown streets run one way so there is always some walking when transferring.

On my first bus trip with DaVida by my side and the bus instructors, I made it all the way up to Group Health for the low vision meeting. The bus instructors asked if I could find my own way to my classroom. I said, "Yes, I think I can." I started to walk forward and along came a very dapper-looking gentleman, obviously sighted as he was walking fast and with a balance in his walk, looking good. I stopped him and asked him if he knew the way to the South building. He responded, "Take my arm and I will lead you there." So I did. Within minutes I was in the South building. I turned around and there were my two instructors and I smiled and said," I did it!"

They said, "You failed, you were supposed to get here by yourself."

"I thought that my job was just to get here, whichever way worked. And besides, wasn't he a cute guy?"

My instructor said, "So was Ted Bundy!" I could have been ashamed but I chose instead to be amused. That was my first day of bus classes. I did get better or rather I became more compliant, but only when my instructors were watching. I still like to ask people for help because it is a way of engaging others and I like to talk to people. I have pretty good radar and usually pick middle-class regular kind of folks.

Phone help is the best part of planning a bus trip. I call the bus service. Tell the attendant the address I am starting from and my goal address. She will give me walking and bus routes to the exact location. This includes which direction to walk when I get off the bus, such as, "Walk ½ block in the direction of the front of the bus, cross the street, left turn, cross the street again, walk ½ block and you will be at the bus stop for the next bus." I received a wallet for bus numbers, so I could hold up the number of the bus I wanted, as more than one bus use each stop. I have never actually used the numbers. When I stand at a bus stop with DaVida, every bus stops and the driver calls out the number of the bus. As we go up the stairs, the driver will tell me where there is a seat. I have never have had to ride standing. Someone always gives me a seat. Even with my anxieties about getting lost we have gone very far on the bus system.

My bus instructor told me how to get to the casino on the other side of Puget Sound. It is practically a straight run from my apartment. I get on the bus across the street and take it to the end of the line. The 16 bus ends at the Bainbridge ferry. I get on the ferry, take a nice little ferry ride, get off the ferry and there is a bus waiting to take me to the casino. The casino bus meets every ferry. Within 15 minutes I can be playing blackjack, DaVida under the table.

Can I see the cards? No. But I have a system. I tell the dealer that I can't see the cards. Since everyone's cards are up, the dealer or sometimes the person just sitting next to me tells me what I have. The only other piece of information I need is what the dealer is showing. Say I have a seven and a four and the dealer has an eight. I double down and usually win. The dealer gives me my winnings in five dollar chips so that I can count them. When I have mixed chips, like green chips which are $25, then I can get mixed up and occasionally make a bet larger than I planned. But once the dealers know my situation they are usually watching out for me. I am so happy at the casino. I feel so empowered being able to get there and play with the help of no one except the dealer. I can come and go, go for lunch, go to the table, and have the best time.

Some of the conversations on the bus are also fun. There is one recurring conversation which is sometimes annoying and sometimes poignant. It goes like this: "What a beautiful dog you have. I had a dog (or cat) and my pet died last year." My own cat, Kitty Anderson, died some years ago. Even now it makes me so sad to think of the death of Kitty, so I empathize with the stories of past and passed pets. I understand the grief. Sometimes, I am in the mood to hear the stories, sometimes not. Another recurring conversation goes on like this:

"What a lovely dog. How old is she?"

I answer.

"What is her name?"

I answer.

"Can I pet her?"

Sometimes I say "Yes." Other times, "No, she's working."

One day I had enough of this repetitive conversation. I turned it around like this:

"What a lovely dog."

"Thanks."

"How old is she?"

I answer her age. "How old are you?"

"You want to know how old I am?"

"Well, yes," I answer.

Then they ask, "What is her name?"

I answer, "DaVida. Do you want to know my name? It's Claire. What is your name?"

"It is Bill."

"So how old are you Bill? Can I pet you?"

We all laugh. It is a nice change from the usual conversation.

My friend Wendy is a driver for Metro. When DaVida sees Wendy in the driver's seat, she licks her and they hug each other. One day we walked onto a bus and the driver looked somewhat like Wendy. DaVida ran over to the driver kissing and wagging. What a surprised driver! That was good for a day's laugh.

CHAPTER 15:

A different kind of prison

DaVida and I regularly visit the Monroe Correctional Institute to participate in a Toastmasters Club meeting for inmates. It is a maximum security facility located northeast of Seattle. At first I went for a four hour orientation with a group of other volunteers. Most of them were from churches or from AA. Mostly I learned that I am not allowed to wear anything that shows skin such as sleeveless shirts or plunging necklines. We're not allowed to wear sandals with bare feet, but sandals with socks are acceptable. But certainly not haute couture! We are not allowed to bring in anything except our driver's license and keys to the car and an asthma inhaler, if needed. We are extremely discouraged from giving anything to inmates, such as cigarettes, ballpoint pens or money.

It's a tiring project to go there. The first time I was picked up at 10:15 a.m. and didn't get home until four p.m. There was an hour drive and then we stopped to eat. We were expected at 12:20 p.m. and you can't get there too early or too late. We parked and went into the first room where we turned over our driver's license for a badge with a picture. We waited in this room with about 40 or 50 other people, mostly relatives of inmates, and when we were called, we went through security. I am not nervous or frightened at the prison. There is so much security and so many guards that it feels safer than a walk in the park.

I went through the metal detector with no problem, but DaVida set off the alarm, as usual, with her harness, leash and metal collar. The guard asked me if she could pat down the dog. I told her the dog would love it. As she was patting down the dog she said, "Is it a female, because if it is a male I will have to call a same-sex guard?"

I said, "If you are patting her down you should be able to tell whether she's a male or female." All the guards thought that was hysterically funny. It seems that this was the first guide dog that ever came in to the prison in the memory of the security guards.

We went down the hall and into a room that was like an elevator. There were sliding doors behind us. When the back doors closed, the front doors opened and then down the hall we went. We went into another room with sliding doors. More walking and we went out of the building and across the very long yard with chain linked fence with barbed wire atop. In this enclosed area I had the thought to let DaVida run loose. We were alone and it was like the paddock in camp. I took off her harness and said, "Go, DaVida!" She took off like greased lightning. Around and around she went. Finally she came back, panting, with a smile on her face. The prison guards saw all this but said nothing. Probably they were looking up "what to do about loose guide dogs" in their prison security manuals. We continued on to another building, past the security guards again, and down the hall into a classroom. That room was the dedicated Toastmasters room with a podium and lots of awards which had been accumulated over the years.

The Toastmasters Club had already been meeting at the penitentiary for many years. Soon the inmates started to drift in. I was surprised that they were wearing chinos and T-shirts or blue jeans. I guess I had been expecting prison outfits. But street clothes looked better. They of course started to pet the dog with my permission. One fellow said that he hadn't petted a dog in 10 years. That made me so sad.

The dog was the hit of the day. She got so much attention and petting and affection. It was so good for the guys and her. There were about 20 inmates and they basically gave motivational speeches and seemed to be working on improving their lives. I was very impressed.

Several important things came out of this meeting for me. I went there out of curiosity and interest in a new experience. I came away with humility and a great feeling that I could give some pleasure by bringing my dog to these incarcerated guys, some of whom will never get out of there. They talked about release dates for those who are eligible, but some are in for life. It was quite the experience for me.

A Toastmaster friend drives once a week and has for several years. I continue to go to the prison as a sponsor for the Toastmasters group. Several of the inmates told me that they count the days until we return. I am honored and humbled by these visits.

The guards came to me after a few wild DaVida runs in the enclosed space and asked me to stop. They gave no explanation. I am behaving now. After all, it is a prison. One must behave!

CHAPTER 16:

Low vision, high tech

There are seven million blind people in the United States. Definitions of "blind" vary from very high partial vision to totally blind. As mentioned my vision is called low partial. I can see large objects like people and furniture but not the details.

A huge market exists for products to aid the blind. Several national organizations and a myriad of local groups are available to aid low vision and blind people. As the boomers age, there will be more and more visually disabled people. At the conventions dozens of companies offer their goods and products for the blind. I love to see the new technology and always have to consider the cost versus benefit.

When I first lost my sight I received some technological aids from the Florida Department for the Blind. They gave me software for my computer which enlarges the screen and reads the text aloud. They also gave me a magnifier called CCTV. This is a piece of equipment somewhat like a microfiche reader. Whatever I place under the light is enlarged on the screen. A button increases or decreases the size of the item. I can look at today's mail or look at a tube to see if it is toothpaste or mayonnaise. It is important for looking at prescription containers. The technology for low visioned people is terrific. I am so thankful to have these aids. The technology for totally blind people is equally impressive ranging from readers to Braille equipment. I especially enjoy showing sighted people my technology and how I manage my life. Folks are so impressed to see how modern technology has progressed to help the blind.

A few miles from my home there is a store that sells products for the blind and low vision public. I have purchased playing cards with large pictures and Braille lettering. Kitchen objects with raised markings are helpful, as well as marked measuring cups and a kitchen timer. I purchase games, lights, talking watches, and many other gadgets. Every large city has a store for the blind.

The Smart Phone is an example of adapted technology. Many blind people use iPhones as they are voice activated, and can take dictation and turn it into text. With every technological advance I think about whether I want it, if I want to learn how to use it, and if I can afford it. No different than for sighted people considering the latest technological marvel and wonder whether it is a necessity or a toy.

My necessities include a cell phone, a talking watch, a talking bathroom scale (a love-hate object), and an audio book player. The book player is available for free from the Library of Congress for anyone who needs it. Thousands (perhaps millions) of audio books are for sale. I suppose if I had to go blind, this is the best time in the history of the world to do so.

I have a computer that reads all the text aloud. It takes dictation and turns vocal words into written text. Some of this book was written that way. The audio player that I spoke of earlier allows me to read a dozen books at a time and the player holds my place in each book. I start a book and get part way through it and get interested in another subject. There are many sites for downloading books, magazines, newspapers, and podcasts. The amount of information and equipment is formidable. I learned to use a service called BARD: Braille and Audio Reading Download Potential, which I was connected to through the

Washington Talking Books and Braille Library service. BARD is part of the library of Congress. The books are downloaded from the BARD site, which has millions of books and magazines. The trick is to download to a place on your computer which you will remember. Then you unzip the book and put it on the Victor. The Victor Reader is basically an iPod for audio readers. It has no screen and all information is sent by audio. I can switch from talking books to Audible books, podcasts, music, notes. Once I choose an area, I can then choose the podcast or book I want to listen to. It holds my place in any book I am reading. One SDS card holds approximately 80 books and hundreds of songs. The only limit is the gigabytes on the cards. It is chargeable and holds a charge for 17 hours. It also can be used for a recorder and can record hundreds of notes. A more recent Victor than mine has more uses. Just like any technical item available, it has more uses and gadgets than I can absorb. I am very happy to be able to take my many books in my pocket and listen as I go. When I am out I hook it up to earphones. At home I hook it up to a speaker system, so I can walk around and cook and do laundry and listen to books. I still love multitasking! Just like everything (skating, cooking, and using a remote) it is easy to do once you practice. It becomes so automatic that it seems mindless.

Many books I want are not available on their site. Members are allowed to download 30 books a month. Evidently I am the only one who feels unfairly limited. I am chomping at the bit waiting for the time to be up, so I can get some more books. This is how I felt as a child when I was allowed to check out only six books at a time from the library. I was so happy to become an adult with no restrictions. One time I ordered over 100 books, when I was doing research. They were delivered to me in cartons from the library. These days, with the Internet, I suppose people don't order books like that anymore. Too bad!

I just finished reading a book called "Crashing Through" which is the true story of a man by the name of Michael May, who is alive today and lives in San Francisco. Michael, after being blind for 44 years, had his vision restored through the use of stem cell surgery. Most of the book is about his trials of trying to adjust to a new life with vision. It is quite an amazing story.

If I win the lottery, I will get some more technology like a GPS for the blind which is also available in the Smart Phone. Another product is a reader that takes a picture and reads the text immediately. This would be good for reading menus and mail that arrives daily. It is possible to be completely independent with the aid of technology. I always love the new helpers, but do not welcome the learning curve as I figure out how to use the latest invention. My computer is enough of a challenge. Some days it is very cooperative. On another day it is like a child having a tantrum. It stops, halts, jumps around, stalls, gasps, starts and stops. Seven or more computer experts have helped me. Some are friends working gratis for hours and hours. Sometimes I hire a "professional," who guarantees success. Several times I have followed the suggestion of the imperative of a new computer. Nothing works. Still the ill-mannered, temper-tantrum computer sits on my desk, misbehaving at will.

CHAPTER 17

Sightless and single

It's all in the details. There is a place for everything and I try to put everything in its place. Sounds easy to you? Or does it sound impossible to you? Both are true. I have a master plan and I know where all my thousands of items live. Then a well-meaning friend comes along to organize…Oh my! I once spent a week looking for the salt. I recently spent five weeks looking for my long scissors. Eventually I found them on the floor next to the night table in the spare bedroom.

It takes about 10 times longer for me to do an average task than it takes a sighted person. I know this as I have studied the situation. When a sighted person is in my kitchen or at my computer doing a job I mentally time the project. Then I measure how long it takes me. It is incredibly frustrating to me as my mind is whirring along. I have adjusted somewhat as the years have passed. Now I forgive myself for my slowness and mistakes. If I drop a stitch in knitting I put it aside until a sighted knitter shows up. There are chunks in the soup. Who cares? I used to be a perfectionist. Knitting perfect garments and preparing the perfect meal were important to me. I gave that up in favor of "good enough" and life has become easier.

Clocks, machines, technology, and equipment are puzzles for me. Marking equipment is one major solution. There are markers that look like the erasers on the back of a pencil. These markers, also called "dots," come in sheets. Pick one off and stick it on the house key. My son Russ marked the flat panel of the microwave. There is a dot on the control panel's "Clear" and one on the numbers 1, 3, and 5. I have dots on the remotes, on the washer and dryer, and even on my post office box. Well, that is until some well-meaning postal employee comes along to clean the bank of post office boxes. Until then I can find my post office box.

My desk looks like a sign-making factory. I can see and read size 150 font. That means a phone number fills one page. You may use post-its, I use giant signs. On my desk right now are giant signs to remind me to go to the cobbler for inserts, some friend's phone numbers, some passwords for shopping online, reminders about the Senior Center, and more.

All of my ointments and medications are labeled individually. These signs took days to prepare, but it was very important and worthwhile. When I want burn ointment I don't want to confuse it with toothpaste or worse. Use your imagination. I use clear sandwich bags. Each has a giant sign in 150 typeset and one tube inside. Some examples are Neosporin, Benadryl cream, band aids, burn ointment, and antihistamine pills. There are probably one hundred little bags in different parts of my home. Some I keep in my purse. Some labels I stick right on boxes, such as aspirin in the medicine cabinet. Lots of items are identifiable simply by touching, for example dental floss, paper clips, rubber bands, stapler, scotch tape, and binder clips. Just close your eyes and try finding items in your desk drawer.

My clothes are organized by items and color, for example all red tops are together. Just by feeling I can tell the difference between a long sleeve silk blouse, a red sweater, a red sweatshirt, or a cotton long sleeve shirt. The difficult part occurs when there are shades of color and some things don't look good together. Blue colors are tricky. My daughter-in-law Aureole helps me figure out what looks good. I clip tops and slacks together. My socks often don't match the outfits. I have given up on caring. A blind friend told me she once went to work with a red shoe and a blue shoe. A sense of humor helps!

Laundry is much easier today than it used to be. Dark clothes do not run anymore. No worries about turning all the underwear pink. I have a system for socks. Every pair has a small pin attached. When I take off my socks, I use the attached safety pin to pin the two together. I have no sock sorting problems. When a single sock shows up, I put it on the top of the bureau until its partner shows up. When I wash bed linens I fold the dry sheets and pillow cases and roll them together in a package. They are much easier to find.

Eating, getting food, and cooking are all one subject for me. I rarely cook, instead I gather food. That includes leftovers from lunch in a restaurant, take-out food delivered to my home, and already cooked food at the supermarket. I can cook when I am in the mood. I can boil water and make spaghetti. It is done when a strand sticks to the wall. I make soup and freeze the leftovers. Cutting up vegetables requires concentration so as to not bleed. Lots of food comes cut up in the supermarket. When I cut cantaloupes and watermelon I find it difficult to get the fruit and not the rind. It is tiring to prepare food. I often eat burritos (frozen, cook three minutes in microwave), or sandwiches. For my good health I drink fruit juice and vegetable juice. So far my life is good.

My refrigerator is as carefully organized as my house. Salad dressing is in the top-right shelf of the door. Jams and condiments are on the left. I can often identify each by shape, smell, or by looking at the label under the CCTV word enlarger. Salad and veggies are on the bottom shelf. Yogurt and cheese are on shelf #2 on the left. When I visit a friend I am helpless to find anything in their refrigerators. A container with a lid is a mystery. Who knows what it is?

My pantry is similarly organized. I always look at cans with the CCTV after some mishaps such as opening green beans when I wanted soup.

I get along quite well, but I could not do it without all of the help from my dear friends who shop for me, thread needles for me, and tell me where they place items.

This forced retirement affords me the time to play with art except for the restriction of terribly bad eyesight. When I was pregnant with my third son Russ I began to paint. With no class or direction I painted colors and swirls, playing with technique I made up. This amateur work led to some needlepoint designs. In short order my business was booming. Sometimes I thought the women who came to buy canvases and yarn were there just to play with the baby. Russ looked liked the Gerber baby — rosy-cheeked and curly blond hair. His most distinctive feature has always been his eyes. Even today, all grown up, he has one brown eye and one blue eye. People stare at him and point to his eyes as if to say "Do you know that you have two different colored eyes?" That may have been what drew all those Long Island women to my house to buy canvas.

Starting to experiment again in my 60s I found the only way to know what I was painting required holding the painting an inch or two from my face. Paint on my nose is the telltale sign I've been creating. I put drop cloths on the desk, floor and even my chair. Still there are paint blotches to be found. No wonder artists have studios. Working in my living room is less than efficient.

The results are questionable. I have no paintings to show off. My friends, club members, and family members take the paintings away as soon as I finish one. Some even pay for the paintings. They may be trying to discourage me. It might be the "Grandma Moses effect." The paintings aren't very good, but isn't it amazing that a partially-sighted woman can paint? So what if the flowers are detached from the stems and the beach doesn't meet the water. As usual for me, I am having fun. Painting puts me in the "zone" where there is no hunger, no time, just self.

Often I switch to knitting which is much cleaner. It used to be fun to knit sweaters, afghans, and complicated designs and stitches. Now I knit blankets with various colors and variegated stripes. It takes months and sometimes years to finish a project. I'm in no hurry. It's the process, not the product that I love. Many of my loved ones have a cover, blanket, or afghan with my nametag affixed on it. Gifting is all the happiness I want.

CHAPTER 18:

Second Half Champion

In 2010, Wells Fargo Investments announced an essay contest about people who had reinvented themselves in the second half of their lives. It was called "Second Half Champions." My dear friend and co-writer of this book, June Brasgalla, wrote an essay about me. It was one of three winners in the State of Washington. It was picked from thousands of entries.

She wrote:

"Claire has been my friend for over 25 years. When I first met her she lived in Miami, Florida, where she led a very busy and productive life. Divorced at an early age with three sons to raise and no guaranteed career, she created for herself a life of productivity.

Her most productive years financially were in her fifties and sixties when she worked as an accountant and was organizing secretary for associations such as Harvard Alumni club, Wharton Alumni club, etc. Her sons were grown and lived far away so Claire made a life for herself in which she was healthy, happy, and had many friends.

However, one day, when she was in her mid sixties, she woke up and she could not see out of one eye. An examination showed that she had had an optical stroke which left her effectively blind. She handled it with aplomb, still driving her big old car around and going to a different group meeting every day or night of the week. Two years later, while driving through New Mexico on vacation, the other eye shut down. Her worst fears realized, she faced life as a legally blind woman.

Since that time, she has moved to Seattle, Washington and started a new life. She can see enough to get around a little and she moved into a home where there was some assistance and meals. She learned the bus system in Seattle and proceeded to get around that city by herself. After a year, she went to Guide Dogs for the Blind camp in California and met her lovely dog, DaVida. The two of them spent a month learning to live together and now they are inseparable.

Claire has never lost her resolve to live life to the fullest. She joined Toastmasters in Seattle and besides the weekly meeting; she goes with the others to a local prison to help the inmates learn public speaking. She connected with the local Mensa group where she began to share her great ideas and penchant for innovative activities with the group and is now running for office as local group leader. She travels alone, a real challenge for a blind woman with a dog. However, she faces each challenge as an adventure and is not shy about accepting help from people who offer it.

She also joined the Speakers' Bureau and with DaVida gives about eight talks a month. Claire is a gifted writer, who has written books and articles about running a business and improving your life. She has a Blog and writes stories about her adventures with DaVida.

She is eager to travel and visit friends and is not afraid of the difficulties that might face her.

She is the consummate friend, and has literally saved lives by her wise counsel and her supportive friendship and availability. No woman I know inspires me more or makes better lemonade than Claire!"

Submitted by June Brasgalla

Sometime later, I was contacted by Wells Fargo. They proposed to prepare a short video about me to go on their web pages. You can still find my story and others on their webpage under 'Second Half Champions."

When they arrived, this is what I told them:

"Here is how I overcame my depression and defeat and found a way to live joyfully. Not everyone chooses to get on with life. I know a number of blind and partially-blind persons who, after years of blindness are still on the sofa, crying, waiting for someone to bring a sandwich. This is the critical choice we make and why the video crew was filling my living room.

In Viktor Frankl's book "Man's Search for Meaning," he writes of how those interred in a concentration camp still had life choices to make. Some shared their meager food with each other. Others stole food from others. We always have choices about how our life will go. I read this book every few years so I can remember to be grateful and to make the most of my life.

Sooner or later, we all wind up face down in the oatmeal. Then all the choices will be over. For now, and until that day, I will get up every day and go out the door to have some fun, help others, enjoy the day and spread love. Hold off on that oatmeal!"

In February 2011, a grand ceremony was held in Benaroya Hall in Seattle for the Wells Fargo presentation to several hundred guests their winners for Washington State's "Second Half Champions." It was a snowy night in Seattle, but the hall was crowded with family, friends and other well-wishers. My family was there, as well as dear friends from far and wide. DaVida and I sat in places of honor on stage at this magnificent performance hall, while presenters announced our names and the videos were shown on a large screen.

Sitting in that theatre for concerts I would never have imagined I would stand on its stage. There I was receiving an award for reinventing myself in the second half of my life. To my blurry eyes, the hall looked like a red velvet and gold box with hundreds of bright marbles. All those people looked like baubles but were actually hundreds of people who came to honor me. This was truly the highest moment of my recent life. Who would ever think that it would come to this? All I did was try to make a life of the shambles it was in when I was literally struck blind. DaVida was likewise so excited to be surrounded by every person she loves. It was a glorious moment for us.

Who would ever think that going blind would turn into a fabulous adventure? Given the opportunity to choose I would never have given up my sight, but I have made the best of it and it has turned out to be wonderful. Let the fabulous adventure continue!

AFTERWORD

Where do you go from here?

My strong advice to you, if you have failing vision, if you are blind, or if you are blessed with full vision, is this: Get a life! Even if you are disabled, poor, unemployed, underemployed, retired, and in pain. Those are not good enough reasons to give up. This applies to almost all older Americans, but there is still hope out there for a full life filled with meaning and happiness.

I speak from my life and not just theory. As you know from reading this book, I was once a successful entrepreneur in good health, managing four of my own businesses, and quietly building an impressive portfolio of real estate properties. I owned or had deposits to purchase thirteen properties. When I had my second optic stroke and lost most of my vision, I was soon faced with choices about how to live the rest of my life.

After my first optic stroke, when I still had vision in one eye, one of my doctors, a Dr. Norman Schatz, was very helpful. He took one of his shoes in his hand and said "Live your life; don't wait for the other shoe to drop." It didn't happen overnight, but that is just what I did. I went back to work, drove, and worked at the computer. I made only two changes to my life. I moved from a condo with a steep staircase to a one-level apartment and that summer I went to Italy to see as much art as I could. I jammed all the living in, because I didn't know how blind I might become.

The next year in August as I was driving on Route 66 in Santa Fe on the way to my niece's wedding reception, the vision in the good eye went blurry. I knew what happened right away. Now I was blind. That was in the summer of 2005. Very soon afterward the real estate market collapsed like a house of cards. In weeks I lost most of my paper fortune, my career, my businesses, my ability to see and my optimistic spirit.

Seven years later, however, I am exhilarated, involved in life, and excited about the future. I still have blurry impaired vision, trouble with my hips and back and now live on a small budget. That is a far cry from where I was a few years ago, but I am at peace, have few nightmares, and my life is good.

I am suggesting to you that if you want a better life, one filled with joy and laughter, you need to be proactive and create a new kind of life for yourself.

If at all possible, do some kind of volunteer work. It might be a simple service, such as calling on elderly people who are lonely and simply talking to them. Or you might offer to feed someone's cat while they are away.

Think creatively — start brainstorming with friends to find your niche.

You will find that you have more to offer than you can ever imagine.

Make a list of your personal talents and see where you might be of service to others. Recent scientific research by the Corporation for National and Community Service has shown a huge connection between volunteering and good health. Volunteers have greater longevity, lower rates of depression and less incidence of heart disease.

I am aware that it is not easy to find a way to serve your community.

It might take a little research and digging. Here's where you may have to ask for help.

I urge you to make a distinction between being self-sufficient and knowing when to ask for help. I was a very independent woman and preferred to "do it myself." I had to learn what things I could do and those things I would have to have done for me. Be ready to accept the unlimited kindness that is offered in this world by people who want to be generous with their time and talent. Don't abuse their kindness, but allow them to help you when they offer.

Most importantly, show your gratitude! If someone gives you transportation, offer to pay for some of their gasoline. If you can't pay much, at least make the offer.

As you become involved in some sort of community volunteer service, you will find that someone depends on you. That's a very empowering feeling! Knowing that your contribution and what you are doing for someone is looked forward to is a great motivation to keep on going.

There are millions of lonely people in nursing homes who have no one to care for them. If you (and possibly your dog) were to choose just one person to visit once a week, imagine how much that person would look forward to your visit! Both of you would benefit.

Perhaps you could go to a local service organization and offer to fold newsletters. Most churches can use this kind of help, and if it is your church, more is better. Perhaps you can hand out programs at a church service or musical performance. Ask the wonderful staff at any local Lighthouse for The Blind for advice and they will surely assist you in your goal for a more meaningful, selfless life.

Life has meaning, if someone or something is reliant on YOU!

Where and what to do? Look at what you love to do and follow that yellow brick road.

Claire and DaVida Visiting

Speaking to groups is my pleasure. This is quite unusual. Some surveys and research results show that most people would rather die instead of talking in front of a live audience. This is a global fears top ten. Fortunately we enjoy audiences. With my audio-visual aide, DaVida, we attend fun and interesting groups. We have appeared in front of elementary school children, teenagers, neighborhood business people, retired citizens. Some of our favorites are "Brownies", kindergarten classes, Rotary, Kiwanis, Elks, writers' clubs, book groups, Networking groups, Chambers of Commerce, Women's Groups, Men's Groups, and all the others.

If you would like Claire and DaVida to appear in front of your group, just contact us.

www.ClaireAnderson.net

Claire@ClaireAnderson.net

Claire Anderson
P.O. Box 17175
Seattle WA 98127

Keep in touch, and Smiling at you,

Claire and DaVida

Count me "In"

Each of us has a story of unexpected triumph. Send me your stories of winning, miracles, and determination. We will compile the stories for publication. Yes, you can be a star for writing the story and your friend or relative can star in a story of strength and grace.

We want to read your story.

Be sure to make a copy as your story won't be returned. We will hold it for future editions.

Send your story via email attachment to Claire@ClaireAnderson.net

Or send your typewritten stories with a SASE (Self Addressed Stamped Envelope) to:

Claire Anderson
P. O. B. 17175
Seattle WA 98127

Keep in touch, smiling at you,
Claire and DaVida

Acknowledgements

New Year's Eve 2011, as the ball dropped in New York, I made a resolution to finish this book in 2012. I had my blog, my journal, and articles in progress all over my computer. My dear best friend June Brasgalla and I decided to pull it into a book and get the story told. I gave June packs of pages which seemed to me like scrambled eggs. Many hours, weeks, and months of work went into this volume. From her clear and outlined brain came this organized book. My first and most important thank you is to my dear best friend June Brasgalla: "Without you this book would never have been published. Thank you from the bottom of my heart."

Many thanks to Kirk Stines, who did the first edit of this book. Kirk inspired me to get going and then keep going.

Peggy Sturdivant founded Ballard Writers Collective and has become my mentor and guide. I am so happy the organization formed just when I needed it to happen. Peggy has introduced me to many people including John Linse, a graphic designer who helped on final production. Peggy is a wonderful "Connector."

Jerry Gay is a Pulitzer Prize winning photographer who photographed DaVida for the front cover. How inventive is he?

Holly Schwartztol, my best friend, was there from the beginning of the story. Holly edited every page, wrote the introduction, and, as a friend, has counseled me for so many years that I am embarrassed to say how long it has been. Many decades is the answer.

Linda Redding, one of my many best friends was on that fateful cruise. She is always there for me, often flying thousands of miles when I need her. Isn't it wonderful to have so many best friends?

Sandy Stein is also my best and dear friend, one of the best listeners and info junkies. Sandy cruised with us to the Bahamas. She edited each word of this book. Thank you so much.

Robert Jaeger has held my computer together with many hours of upgrading and support. Muchas gracias.

Bev Lefcourt was my first friend to meet DaVida and hostess extraordinaire

Irene Yovu is my dear best friend and most interesting dog walker. Irene was in the car when I lost my sight. It was she who walked the dog onto that fateful Astroturf on our Bahamas cruise.

Bedstemor Else Hagen is DaVida's grandma and morning friend and an angel to me. My life is enhanced every sleepy morning when Else arrives at my door, smiling in spite of the rain, to walk herself and DaVida. Else has convinced me of the Norway saying, "There is no such thing as bad weather: there is only poorly dressed."

Alco Canfield started as my Braille teacher and ended as best friend. She tutored me to be an independent and happy blind person. That's quite a good trick.

Emma McAdams is another angel in my life; helper, computer aide, and friend. It was Emma who read each edit from all my dear friends and painstakingly incorporated them into the main documents.

Java Bean Coffee shop has been there for morning friendliness. It feels like "Cheers" where everyone knows my name.

Virginia Johnson is my dear friend and secretary. She has handled the myriad of issues of life such as bills, insurance forms, and taxes so I could devote myself to writing this book.

Special thank yous to Ellen Casey, Steve Lent and Bob Brideson who have encouraged in this project, never letting me give up. Thank you dearly.

Lastly I thank my family – Aureole & Russ, Brian, Scott, Greta Sorenson & Peter Wallis, and my grandchildren who have been supporting this effort, ever-confident that I would finish it. I did!

It's a good thing that writers get more space than Oscar winners. It takes a community to write a book.

June Brasgalla

June Brasgalla was a Master Teacher in the State of Florida and Teacher of the Year Finalist for Broward County, Florida in 1989. During her teaching career, she wrote human interest and stories related to educating and raising children. She is credited with articles in Solares Hill, a newspaper in Key West now called The Citizen, a Burnt-Hills, New York regional newspaper, the Ft. Lauderdale Herald Tribune, the National Mensa Bulletin and the national PTA journal.

She wrote a grant-writing booklet used by Advantage Learning Systems which was the most requested piece of support literature ever offered by the company, now known as Renaissance Learning, Inc.

In retirement, she dedicates herself to writing and has published a biography of an iconic Key West woman entitled, "Teena Rice: la Reina." She is currently working on both a family history book and a novel set in Southern West Virginia.

Claire Anderson

Claire has been writing since she was a child. In college she wrote for her college newspaper and was editor of the yearbook. After graduating with an English degree and as a new teacher she gathered together a grammar text to help her students understand fundamentals. Some years later she wrote one of the earliest books on "Working from your Home" which had a successful run for years. In the 70s she published a newsletter about metaphysics with Holly Schwartzol called "Transcending Limits." Shortly after that Claire wrote "Spiritualism and Healing as a Business" to help healers think profitably. "Sightless in Seattle: Adventures with my Guide Dog" has been Claire's dream fulfilled. Claire lives in Seattle with DaVida and in close contact with many friends and family. This is happiness!

15198123R00089

Made in the USA
Charleston, SC
22 October 2012